GOLF
FOR SENIORS

The scenic Millwood Resort golf course, designed by Bob Charles, at Queenstown in the South Island of New Zealand.

GOLF
FOR SENIORS

Bob Charles

With David Pirie

Foreword by

Gary Player

PELICAN PUBLISHING COMPANY
Gretna 1994

Published simultaneously in October 1994 by
   Pelican Publishing Company, Inc., in North America
   David Bateman Ltd. in New Zealand
   Aurum Press Limited in the United Kingdom
   Thomas C. Lothian Pty Ltd in Australia

ISBN 1-56554-111-1

Designed by Steve Henderson

Printed in China through Colorcraft Ltd.
Published by Pelican Publishing Company, Inc.
1101 Monroe Street, Gretna, Louisiana 70053

CONTENTS

Foreword by Gary Player

Introduction   7

Chapter 1
The Grip   9

Chapter 2
Stance (address) and ball position   15

Chapter 3
The Swing   25

Chapter 4
Swing sequence   37

Chapter 5
Swing drills   55

Chapter 6
Bunker shots/sand traps   63

Chapter 7
Pitching and chipping   73

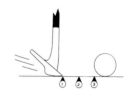

Chapter 8
Putting   83

Chapter 9
Difficult shots   93

Chapter 10
Faults   104

Chapter 11
Percentage shots, tactics and
the mental game, practice,
the teaching professional   111

Chapter 12
Equipment   115

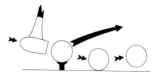

Glossary of golfing terminology   119

Index   122

PUBLISHER'S NOTE

To the best of our knowledge, this book is unique in two respects:

1. It is the first to be written specially for *Senior Golfers*, or *Seasoned Golfers* as that great teacher Harvey Penick refers to such players in his *Little Red Book*. By senior golfers we do not refer specifically to those who play the professional senior circuit, but to the thousands and thousands of people who take up the game in later life, or who continue to play it despite the eroding effects of the human ageing process. Thus it makes allowance for stiff joints and weakening muscles, and shows how concentration on accuracy and the use of wise grey cells can overcome the disadvantage of any loss of distance or staying power.

2. It caters for both left- and right-handed players by use of the following simple terminology which applies to both:

TOP HAND and BOTTOM HAND instead of LEFT HAND and RIGHT HAND.

BACK ARM, SHOULDER AND LEG and FRONT ARM, SHOULDER AND LEG instead of LEFT and RIGHT (see diagram below).

Bob Charles is a left-handed player so we have augmented the many illustrations of him demonstrating strokes with those of the right-handed teaching professional, David Pirie, of Clydebank and District Golf Club in Scotland, who has assisted with this book, and the two senior golfers who kindly agreed to be photographed showing how they do it. We believe we have eliminated any confusion that may arise for either a left- or right-hander reading this book.

Since joining the senior circuit some ten years ago, Bob Charles has become one of its most successful players, amongst a galaxy of former stars including Jack Nicklaus and Gary Player, and he has won the Senior British Open twice — in 1989 and 1993. Consequently, he is particularly well qualified to advise his golfing contemporaries, whatever their experience or standard of play may be.

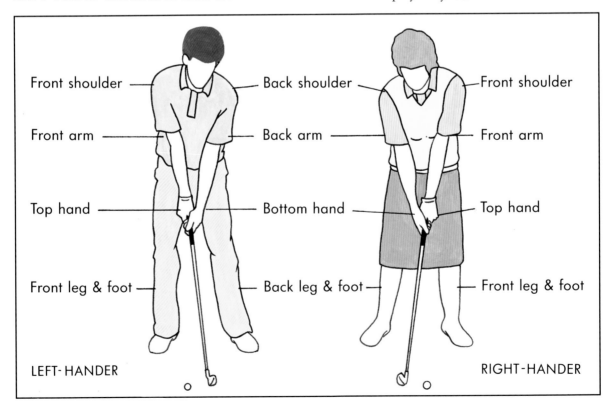

Front shoulder — — Back shoulder — — Front shoulder

Front arm — — Back arm — — Front arm

Top hand — — Bottom hand — — Top hand

Front leg & foot — — Back leg & foot — — Front leg & foot

LEFT-HANDER · RIGHT-HANDER

INTRODUCTION

Bob Charles after winning the British Senior Open Championship for the second time, at Royal Lytham and St. Anne's Golf Club in 1993.

It is an honour and a great pleasure to have this opportunity to write about Bob Charles, the golfer and the man.

I have known Bob and his lovely wife Verity for nearly 40 years and it has indeed been an enriching experience for me and my entire family. Bob has always been a true gentleman, an outstanding father and a loyal husband — attributes that are sorely missing in society today. My wife, Vivienne, went to school with Verity, who served as maid of honour at our wedding. I believe Bob is such a successful person because he has built his life around honesty, both on and off the golf course.

As a player, there is no doubt that Bob is the greatest left-handed golfer of all time. His Regular TOUR record includes five victories, but the highlight of his 'first' golfing career was his victory at the 1963 British Open. In his second career on the Senior TOUR, Bob's record is truly outstanding. Entering the 1994 season, he has won 21 times, including at least one victory each year since 1987. He was the first Senior player to eclipse the $3 million mark, then $4 million and he holds the top spot on the Senior TOUR career money list. Amazingly, since joining the Senior TOUR in 1986 Bob has never been out of the top 10 in season-end earnings. In 1994 he won his third Byron Nelson Trophy for low stroke average, but low scoring is only part of Bob's game.

I believe Bob is a better golfer today than when he won the British Open. He is one of the hardest workers anywhere, and his commitment to excellence is evident in his accomplishment.

Not only is Bob an excellent ambassador for golf, but also for his native country, New Zealand. Bob is very positive about his homeland — a trait that I admire — and is an example to his fellow countrymen that they can succeed as professional golfers if they are diligent.

I am very impressed with this book because it is as useful to those that play right-handed as to lefties. This is not a left-handed analysis of the game; it is a study of the game as a golfer. This book describes Bob's enviable attributes; his ability to drive the ball, his thought processes and his outstanding putting. Every golfer will take away something positive from this edition.

Enjoy this book, and it's a privilege to know Bob and be involved in this special project.

Gary Player

Chapter 1

THE GRIP

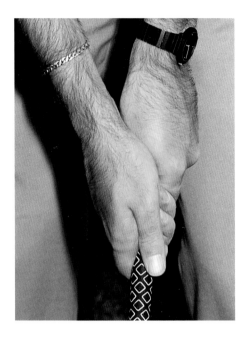

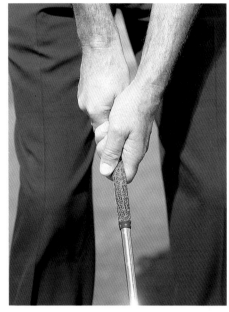

This aspect of the game is probably the most important. How you grip the golf club determines how the clubface will return to the ball on impact.

Grip methods

There are three main ways of holding the club which affect how the bottom hand is placed:
(1) the Vardon or overlapping grip;
(2) the interlocking grip;
(3) the double-handed or baseball grip.

The overlapping or Vardon method is the most popular and is made by placing the small finger of the bottom hand over the index finger of the top hand.

With the interlocking grip, the small finger of the bottom hand is intertwined with the index finger of the top hand.

The baseball method has all the fingers of the bottom hand placed on the golf club with no gap between the hands.

Let us assume that you choose the orthodox Vardon method.

Top hand (left hand for right-handers, right hand for lefties.)

Place the top hand on the golf club first, with the pad or heel of your palm close to the end of the grip. Think of shaking hands with the club. The grip should run across the base of the fingers, with the pad or heel of the hand placed directly on top of the shaft. Usually, the thumb should sit comfortably, just behind centre. The more the thumb is extended the more the grip will be felt in the palm of the hand. The less the thumb is extended the more the grip will be felt in the fingers. I extend my top hand thumb down the centre of the grip (the long thumb grip), which gives me greater control of the club at the top

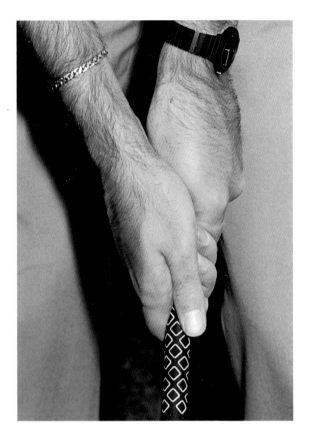

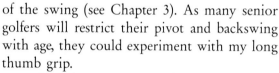

Bob Charles demonstrates the popular overlapping or Vardon grip. This is made by placing the little finger of the bottom hand over the index finger of the top hand.

Left: *A right-handed orthodox overlapping grip.*

of the swing (see Chapter 3). As many senior golfers will restrict their pivot and backswing with age, they could experiment with my long thumb grip.

Looking down, you should be able to see three or four knuckles on your top hand and the 'V' formed by the thumb and index finger should point directly towards your chin or back shoulder. *Bottom hand (right hand for right-handers, left hand for lefties)*

Place the bottom hand with the heel of the thumb over the other thumb, the little finger overlapping the index finger of the top hand. Grip the shaft with the other three fingers by curling them round it. Correctly positioned, this produces a second 'V' between thumb and forefinger which should also point towards the back shoulder. The back of the bottom hand should face directly away from the target.

Both hands

Your hands should work together as one unit on the golf club, both with equal, light pressure to maintain a good feel of the clubhead.

Do not hold the club too tightly. If you do, tension is introduced with disastrous effects on the path of the swing. Just take a firm, natural position with both hands on the club in an easy, light grip. You should not increase pressure or allow any tension to occur. The key is for the grip to be the same as you enter the hitting area as it was at address.

Throughout my career I have used the same basic grip to guide the clubhead in the correct arc and at controlled speed to the ball in all circumstances; to 'feel' the ball, as many top players say, the grip has to be constant. To

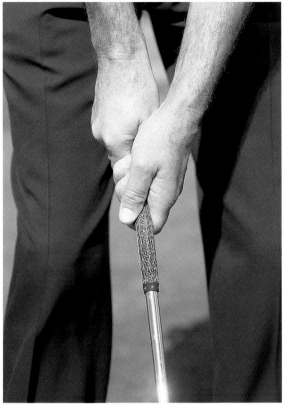

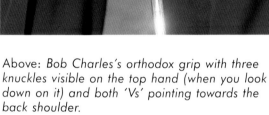

Above: *Bob Charles's orthodox grip with three knuckles visible on the top hand (when you look down on it) and both 'Vs' pointing towards the back shoulder.*

Above right & right: *Note how relaxed the grip is in these fore and aft photographs, yet the hands are obviously going to control the club by working together.*

deliberately slice or hook, alter your stance (see Chapter 9) but *never* your grip, unless forced to by arthritis or some other physical problem.

If you do not hold the club correctly, you will not develop a consistent game. The grip may feel strange or uncomfortable at first but, whenever you have the opportunity, pick up a club, grip it correctly, and it will soon feel natural.

A senior player using a baseball style grip; three knuckles are visible on the top hand; all bottom hand fingers grip the club. Hands are close together but without overlap of index and little finger; both 'Vs' pointing towards the back shoulder. A good strong grip favoured by some golfers.

A senior lady's orthodox overlapping Vardon grip with three top hand knuckles visible and both 'Vs' pointing to the back shoulder.

A weak grip, with barely one knuckle visible on the top hand, places too much strain on the wrist and forearm.

A similar weak grip demonstrated by a senior lady. The result would be a slice.

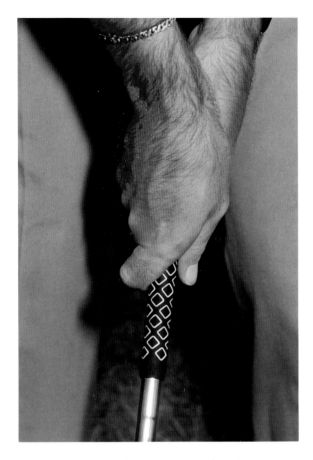

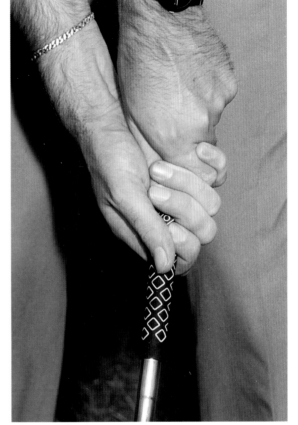

This typical weak 'slicer's' grip has barely one knuckle showing on the front hand and both 'Vs' are pointing to the front shoulder.

A typical strong 'hooker's' grip; four plus knuckles visible on the top hand and both 'Vs' pointing past the back shoulder.

Changing the grip

Many senior golfers have to change their grip slightly due to arthritis or some similar ailment as they advance in years. One of the most common changes is to have slightly thicker (jumbo) grips fitted. This helps the hands fit around the club and, because the grip is thicker, reduces the hand and wrist action and puts slightly more emphasis on the correct body action.

However, if the golfer suffers from a restricted body pivot, then he or she can have thinner grips fitted, putting more emphasis on the hand and wrist action as the club nestles more into the fingers of the hand.

Summary — grip

1. Show at least three knuckles on top hand.
2. Check both 'Vs' point directly towards back shoulder.
3. Back of bottom hand facing directly away from target.
4. Don't grip club too tightly.
5. Both hands work smoothly together to guide arc and speed of clubhead.
6. Grip should be the same at impact with the ball as at address.
7. Once you have mastered the correct grip for you, *never change it (unless a physical condition leaves no choice).*

Chapter 2

STANCE (ADDRESS) AND BALL POSITION

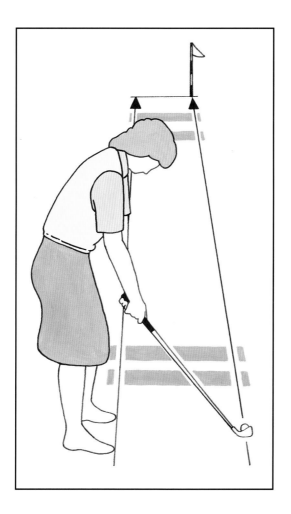

The clubhead, ball and target should be on one line, square to the hips, shoulders and feet on the other line.

Alignment

Many golfers believe that lines drawn across the toes and shoulders should point directly at the target; this is not the case. Think of standing on railway lines: the clubhead, ball and target on one line and the player's shoulders, feet and hips on the other line. This will ensure that you are lined up correctly.

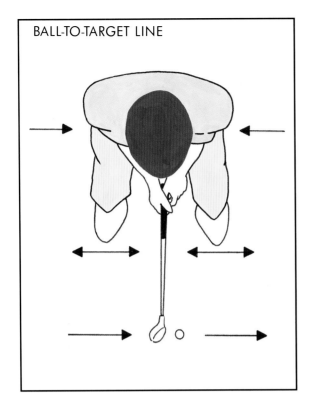

BALL-TO-TARGET LINE

The square stance

Having established that mental image, it is simple to understand what I believe to be the most important fundamental to the development of a solid, reliable swing — *a square stance* — feet, knees, hips and shoulders square to each other and parallel to the ball-to-target line. Concentrate and work on setting up in this way until you do it almost without thinking about it.

The square stance: feet, knees, hips and shoulders square to each other and parallel to the ball-to-target line.

Body posture

To swing the golf club in a smooth, coordinated and relaxed manner, it is absolutely essential to establish the correct body posture at address.

This can be achieved by standing upright with your legs straight, and then simply holding the club out at arms' length with the clubhead at face height. Lean forward from your waist and lower your arms until the clubhead is resting on the ground.

This will set the correct spinal angle for you. Flex both knees a little and keep your chin off your chest. Now you should be comfortably relaxed with the correct body posture.

The address position using a 5 iron. Feet, hips and shoulders are parallel to the ball-to-target line. Chin slightly tilted, up and off the chest.

Looking towards and back from the target, and front on. Note how the chin is raised, creating space for the shoulders to turn correctly. Feet, knees, hips and shoulders are square to each other and parallel to the line of flight. Arms and hands are relaxed and knees slightly flexed.

Summary — stance

1. Establish a square stance.
2. Ball and clubhead on line to target.
3. Shoulder, feet and hips parallel to the ball-to-target line.
4. Bend forward from the waist, knees flexed, chin off your chest.

Above & above left: *Good posture from both these senior golfers using 7 irons; freely hanging arms, slight flexing of both knees, chin high for free follow-through — no hint of 'head down', which must be avoided.*

To help achieve body posture, place the ball the right distance from you and stand erect with legs straight. Hold the club out at arms' length and then lower it to the ground, flexing knees and ensuring arms hang freely. Body posture and ball position should now be correct. To check ball position, carry out the exercise illustrated opposite.

Changing the stance

The stance adopted by senior golfers may have to be slightly changed from that of their more youthful counterparts. The most notable, perhaps, being due to a 'slight thickening' around the waist. If this is the case, stick your bottom out more and let your arms and elbows hang slightly further apart.

This will create space for the arms to turn freely on the backswing. Pay particular attention to your weight distribution and try not to set too much weight on your toes at address as this will result in loss of balance and limited leg action during the swing.

If you are supple enough, you can turn to your advantage any extra weight that may have gained in recent years because you will have more mass behind the spot, providing you concentrate on good weight transference throughout the swing.

Distance from the ball

Having established your grip, body alignment and posture, you have to judge what distance you should be from the ball. There is a simple way to achieve this: with knees slightly flexed and your body leaning over from the waist, drop your golf club onto your front leg. The butt end of the grip should rest approximately 7-10 inches (18-25 cm) above the knee. This test applies to *all* your clubs, and takes into account the different lengths of golf clubs in a normal matched set. Check your position as you read this. If the club falls on your knee, then you are standing too far away from the ball; if the club falls at the top of your thigh, then you are standing too close.

Also, check your weight distribution to make sure your weight is evenly distributed between heels and toes and between front and back foot.

Summary — distance from ball

1. Stand upright, legs straight. Hold club at arms' length; clubhead at face height.
2. Lean forward from waist; lower arms until clubhead rests on its sole.
3. Bend knees slightly; keep chin off your chest.
4. All clubs: check distance from ball by dropping club grip on front leg; butt end should fall 7-10 inches (18-25 cm) above knee.
5. Check weight is evenly distributed.

Above: *Checking the correct distance from the ball using a driver. Note how the butt end of the grip falls 7–10 inches (18–25 cm) above the front knee.*
Right: *The butt end of the grip falls in the same place on the leg when using a number 9 iron.*

Correct ball position

Like many top tournament players, I play the ball from a point opposite the front foot heel to the centre of my stance depending on the club being used. The tee shots and long shots off the fairway should be played off the front heel and shorter clubs back towards the centre.

The position of the ball plays a vital part in allowing the club to meet the ball at the right stage of the golf swing. When using irons, this is at the bottom of the arc of the swing; in wood shots, it is slightly on the upswing, which produces a sweeping motion rather than a descending blow.

Later in the book I will describe some simple drills for establishing the correct ball position.

The correct ball position for all tee shots is opposite the front heel. For long and medium irons off the fairway it should be behind the heel and towards the centre.

Fairway woods

Many golfers experience difficulty with the fairway woods, mainly due to lack of confidence in their ability to get the ball airborne. This is usually because the ball position at address is too far forward, so that the clubhead is rising as it makes contact, producing topped or excessively low shots. Depending upon the lie, position yourself so the ball is at a point just inside your front heel.

Some older golfers carry a 4, 5, or even a 7 wood in their bag. These clubs, having plenty of loft, inspire confidence. They are also extremely useful from the semi-rough as they cut through the grass more effectively than a long or medium iron.

Remember that practice makes perfect. If you have a struggle with these clubs, spend some time on them until you master them. Your fear of fairway goods will soon be overcome.

Note the different ball positions for fairway shots. If the ball is lying well, as on a well watered, lush fairway, it could be played from a point between the front heel and the centre of your stance. If the lie is not so good you may have to position it further back in your stance.

Ball position using a 7 wood off the fairway — slightly front of centre. A very useful club for senior golfers.

Correct ball position for a 7 iron shot — slightly front of centre.

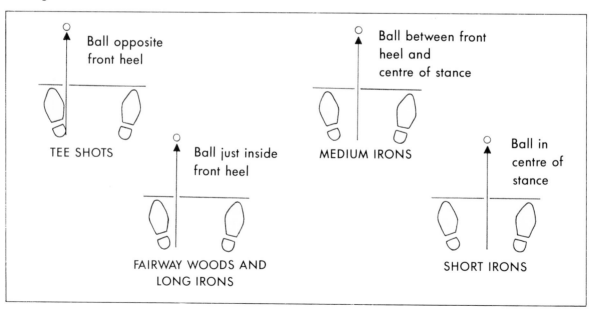

Ball opposite front heel

TEE SHOTS

Ball just inside front heel

FAIRWAY WOODS AND LONG IRONS

Ball between front heel and centre of stance

MEDIUM IRONS

Ball in centre of stance

SHORT IRONS

Summary — ball position

1. Tee shots: ball opposite front heel.
2. Fairway woods: just inside front heel.
3. Long irons: just inside front heel.
4. Medium irons: between front heel and centre of stance.
5. Short irons: centre of stance.

The orthodox stance for a woman golfer is the same as for a man. For this tee shot, the ball is correctly positioned opposite the front heel and the elbows are set fairly close together with no tension in legs, hands or arms.

A medium iron off the fairway; ball positioned between front heel and centre of stance, arms relaxed, knees flexed and chin up.

Chapter 3

THE SWING

Backswing

The start of the backswing, or 'takeaway', involves moving the clubhead, hands and arms in unison back from the ball, with the shoulders turning simultaneously to create one movement which takes the clubhead straight back in line with the target. If you are tall, like me, the plane of the swing will probably be upright (or close to it); if shorter, then the plane can be flatter and slightly inside the line to the target.

But remember to 'feel' the club with the hands all the way and *not to grip tightly.* Keep the back elbow tucked in close to the side until you near the top of the swing. If your pivot is restricted and you are forced to play with a very short backswing, keep your back elbow tucked in throughout. The front arm should be kept as straight as possible as far back in the swing as you are physically able.

Allow your body weight to shift onto the back foot. At the halfway point of the backswing, the hands will be waist high, the golf club should be a straight extension of the front arm, and the back of the front hand should be parallel to the ball-to-target line.

Now the wrists can start to cock, but must not take the club from its correct plane. As the shoulders continue to turn, the arms should swing the golf club up to the top of the backswing. Try to feel as if your upper inner front arm is 'hugging' your chest as this ensures that your arm and body action remain 'connected' during the backswing.

If you can manage a full swing, by now the front knee is pointing directly behind the ball towards the back knee, which should still be slightly flexed — just as it was when you set up. The shoulders have turned through 90 degrees and the hips through 45 degrees. These movements probably will have lifted the front heel off the ground preventing restriction at the top of the backswing. This usually happens with long woods and irons and it is especially recommended for golfers with restricted swings to aid hip and shoulder turn, but is not necessary for short clubs. Most weight will transfer to the inside of the back leg.

If you cannot manage a full backswing, it doesn't matter too much because you can still hit the ball long and straight, even if you stop your swing threequarters of the way back. In fact this gives some golfers greater accuracy because there is less danger of getting out of the correct swing plane and, as the wrists have already started to cock, there will be plenty of clubhead speed when they are uncocked just before impact.

There are several other important factors. At the top of your backswing make sure both thumbs are under the shaft and that the shaft is above the back shoulder, pointing directly at the target; or with the short back swing, thumbs and shaft are pointing at the sky with the vertical shaft directly in line with the target and on the correct plane. If you are supple enough, your back will be pointing towards the target. With both full and short backswings, most of your weight will have transferred to the inside of your back leg.

Try to keep your head still. However, allowing it to swivel back slightly, whilst keeping the neck in the same vertical position, will help to create the rotation required during the backswing. But, keep both eyes riveted on the ball — this is essential to prevent swinging back too far or moving your head back too much. At the top of your backswing, if you can only see the ball with one eye you will have done either one or both those things with disastrous results to your shot.

At this point, give some thought to the speed of your backswing, or swing tempo. Remember, more errors are caused by swinging too fast than too slowly. So use a smooth, slow tempo in the backswing.

Summary — backswing

The main points to remember in the backswing are:

1. From square, relaxed stance initiate smooth, straight back, takeaway of clubhead by moving hands and arms together as one. *Do not grip tightly.*
2. Mid-way, with hands at waist height, club is extended straight back on target line almost parallel to the ground; immediately after, wrist-cock begins.
3. Torso turns, responding in unison to 1 and weight begins to transfer to back leg.
4. Shoulders, knees and hips wind up like a spring in unison with clubhead, hands and arms.
5. At top of backswing, shoulders have turned 90 degrees — or less with a short backswing. Front knee is pointing towards or behind the ball.
6. Wrists cocked to set club parallel to ball-to-target line in full swing, near vertical but in line with target in short swing.
7. Reasonably straight front arm throughout backswing.
8. Maintain constant spinal and neck angle, *head as still as possible. Keep chin off chest, both eyes on the ball.*
9. Smooth, slow tempo.

In this backswing sequence 1–4, note how Bob Charles extends the arm and club straight back on the target line to waist height. The body then turns, pivots and weight is transferred to the back leg at the top of the backswing. Note: perfect balance and sense of rhythm throughout.

1

2

3

4

Downswing

There are many theories about the correct way to initiate the downswing.

One recommended by many very good teaching professionals is to visualise the sequence starting from the ground up. So if you have raised your front heel during the backswing, your first move is to move your front knee back to its original starting position. This will, in turn, plant your heel back onto the ground. By now, you will have started a chain reaction through the hips to the arms, particularly the back arm, dropping them down. This ensures that your back elbow brushes past your back hip. At this point, your body will still be facing the ball. Now turn your waist towards the target which will promote the feeling of the clubhead being pulled through the impact zone by the unwinding action of the torso.

On impact the clubhead will be released squarely by the hands onto the back of the ball. Do not grip the club too tightly as this will 'choke' the releasing/firing action of the hands and clubhead, resulting in a slice.

Personally, I prefer not to think of any one movement starting everything off. Hands, arms, shoulders, torso, legs and feet, must all move in unison in the downswing as they must in the backswing. Therefore, I think about getting the clubhead square and smoothly to the ball at impact and concentrate on pulling down the hands, arms and shoulders to achieve that. If you need to focus on one movement, perhaps the hips, to get everything going, that's fine. But remember, it is only a means to an end to get everything co-ordinated and working together. Here are some tips that may help you achieve that:

• Coming into the impact area, be sure the back elbow brushes the hip to retain the correct swing-plane and that the clubhead is square to the ball at impact. This will enable you to keep the back shoulder down and behind the ball for as long as possible which, in turn, will help stop the shoulders turning away from the target line before impact, thus causing a hook or slice.

• Try not to hit from the top of the swing. In

1

2

3

other words, don't attempt to explode with all the force you can muster from the very start as a sprinter would explode from his blocks; accelerate smoothly with the object of achieving maximum clubhead speed at impact. Some golfers find it easier to do this if they pause slightly between the completion of the backswing and the start of the downswing. If you do, pause only momentarily or you will freeze, cramp up and lose your rhythm.

• To achieve distance, keep the hands ahead of the clubhead into the impact area, but do not let either hand dominate the shot; the front hand guides the club, the back hand does the hitting, but both must work equally together. If they don't, the result will be either a late hit (too much front hand) causing a slice, or an early hit (too much back hand) causing a hook.

• Distance is also dependent on a power equation which is created by two factors: (a) clubhead speed maximised by the uncocking of the wrists which should begin as the club shaft is about parallel to the ground; and (b) the transfer of body weight to the front foot which is occurring rapidly at the same time. **So — weight transfer plus clubhead speed = power.**

Follow-through

The follow-through should be a natural continuation from the downswing, extending the arms and club directly towards the target for as long as possible. Try to achieve the following:

• Keep your eyes on the spot where the ball was hit for as long as possible into the follow-through.

• Wherever you finish the follow-through, it is essential you are well balanced and following the flight of the ball to the target. To do this, all

4

In these different shots 1–3, Bob Charles demonstrates how, in the downswing, the hands, arms, shoulders, torso, hips, legs and feet coordinate in unison to create one movement to get the clubhead square and smoothly to the ball at impact. In shot 4, note in particular the back elbow brushing the hip just before impact, the still head and the hands ahead of the ball at impact.

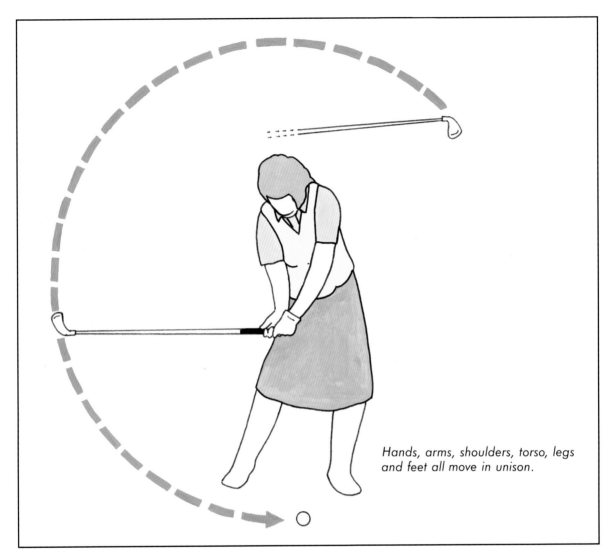

Hands, arms, shoulders, torso, legs and feet all move in unison.

weight should be on the front foot and just the toes of the back foot (the ballerina position) to maintain balance. If the back foot remains anchored to the ground, you will be off balance and will probably have sliced. Certainly you will not have achieved the proper power equation because your weight will not have transferred fully from back foot to front foot.

• Keep your front side firm and try to feel that you are hitting against it.

• The back arm, which should have been almost straight at impact, should remain so for at least three-quarters of the follow-through. This makes it easier to keep the clubhead square to the ball at impact and to 'throw' the hands, arms and club

straight at the target after the ball.

• The head should stay still, with the eyes on where the ball was. The momentum of the swing will force the head up as the hips and shoulders turn or pivot. At the same time the front arm will begin to bend. Try to keep the back arm reasonably straight until you are forced to let it wrap round your shoulders in order to get your stomach and chest square to the target. This is how they should be on completion of the follow-through.

• If you can't complete the full follow-through pivot, concentrate on the straight extension of arms and club towards the target as far as you are physically able, keeping the back arm more or

Above & left: *The follow-through from front on, front side firm, back arm straight almost to top of swing, eyes on where the ball was to well after impact (see below). The head is still until forced up by the momentum as hips and shoulders pivot, weight on front foot and only toes of back foot on the ground. Note the full extension of hands, arms and club towards target for as long as possible.*

less straight and finishing with the club shaft at roughly 45 degrees from the ground.

The momentum created by unwinding the body will ensure that the clubhead is catapulted towards the target, eventually finishing up above the front shoulder with the entire body weight on the outside of the front foot and the stomach and chest facing the target. The back foot will be in a ballerina position, with the toes on the ground and the sole of the foot facing directly away from the target. You should now be fully relaxed and balanced.

Get the feeling of swinging the club and accelerating the clubhead through the ball. Do not swing at the ball, swing through it.

Left: The follow-through looking towards the target. Eyes have remained on the impact point for as long as possible and the head only starts to turn as the forearms and hands travel well above the shoulders; weight is transferring rhythmically onto the front leg. Note the full shoulder turn and perfect balance.

Above: Possibly the worst advice you could get is 'Keep your head down'. As you can see, it would now be almost impossible to turn the shoulders freely in the golf swing as weight remains on the back foot. The advice should be to keep your head still and watch the ball.

Changes to the swing

Here are some tips that may help golfers who cannot manage to turn the shoulders through 90 degrees during the backswing.

The takeaway, as described in this chapter, should be relatively 'age proof' but when you reach the halfway point of the backswing, think of 'thumbs up' to the sky. This will create height in the backswing and keep the swing in the correct plane — that is, not too flat or too upright, according to your build and height.

Don't worry if you can't make the full shoulder turn — as long as your thumbs are swinging up, you will create the necessary wrist cock and keep the club swinging on the correct plane.

You may find it easier to start the transfer of weight from back to front side during the downswing by moving your front knee towards the target. For you, this may initiate the correct, unified, chain reaction sequence.

However, if you are not supple enough to put emphasis on the body action, you will have to think more in terms of hand and wrist action, making sure you do not grip the club too tightly as this will severely restrict the firing or releasing action of your hands.

After impact, try to feel that your thumbs are again swinging to the sky, having first extended your arms and club directly towards the target as far as possible.

This will enable your swing to be completed with the club shaft finishing above your front shoulder, perhaps vertical, or within 25 degrees or so either side of vertical. Your torso will probably be about 45 degrees to the target rather than facing it, but this will save your spine from the strain of a full pivot as it won't be pulled round by your back arm wrapping round the shoulders and neck to produce the classic follow-through.

Providing you finish properly balanced and in the correct plane, and the club was square to the ball on impact, your ball will still fly straight to the target. You may lose distance but you will not lose accuracy — you may even gain some!

Finally, I would recommend that you take perhaps one more club (loftwise) and swing well within yourself.

Important — if you wear bifocal glasses, don't use them to play golf. Because it is necessary to look down through the bottom section of the lens, the golfer is required to keep his or her head down more than necessary.

This severely restricts the freedom required for turning the shoulders during the backswing and downswing. Nowadays, I believe 'progressive lens' are available; these are much better (so I am reliably informed) as they allow the golfer to see the ball at address without having to keep the head down too much. Also, after impact, when the head is lifted they can follow the flight of the ball. Talk to your optician!

Do we need the perfect swing?

I believe most golfers would love to have the perfect swing. But wait a minute, what is the perfect swing? Who has the perfect swing? You only need to look at the different swings of today's top world stars to quickly realise that, in fact, they all swing the club slightly differently according to their own particular body shape and physique. So if you are a short, fat person, the chances of your swing being moulded along the same lines as mine are fairly remote! Instead, you must develop an individual style that works for you and you alone.

Some players may have a back problem which restricts their movement, but, while this may be a slight handicap, they can learn through lessons and practice that by using more hand and wrist action they can still hit the ball reasonably well and derive just as much pleasure from the game as someone who can swing freely. I know a man, now in his mid-sixties, who suffered a bad back injury playing rugby for his University. His backswing always stops with his hands no higher than his waist. Yet he drives 220-230 yards (200-210 m) consistently and accurately, and plays off an 11 handicap.

Naturally, as one becomes older the golfing muscles will tend to tighten up, but by trying some of the swing exercises described in Chapter 5 you can keep those muscles in good shape. Remember that the golfer who hits the ball the longest distance doesn't necessarily win all the trophies! Golf is a game primarily about accuracy rather than distance and this is why some older players, when less agile, can still play accurate shots to the pin and win their fair share of club trophies at the end of the season. Golf is a game for life.

Most women golfers have less physical strength than their male counterparts but they are often superior in their short game. They have more feel and control in their hands and wrists, so chipping and putting can be considered their greatest strength.

Make sure your basics are sound — the grip, ball position, body alignment and posture — and then if your swing isn't perfect, the chances are you will still be able to play some great shots. At the end of the day, golf is a game to be enjoyed.

Summary — downswing and follow-through

The main points to remember in the downswing and follow-through are:

1. Don't grip the club too tightly.
2. Start a smooth, unified movement of hands, arms, shoulders, hips and legs to get the clubhead square to the ball.
3. Back elbow drops down to brush the hip.
4. Both hands work equally together — front to guide, back to hit.
5. For distance, keep hands ahead of clubhead in impact area.
6. For power, transfer weight from back to front, and maximise clubhead speed by uncocking wrists as you enter the impact area.
7. Head still and glue both eyes on ball to impact, and on impact position, until club is about parallel to ground on follow-through.
8. Fully extend hands, arms and club directly towards target.
9. Finish in maximum unwound position you can manage, with weight fully transferred to front foot and only toes of back foot on the ground.

Chapter 4

SWING SEQUENCE

TEE SHOTS

The driver

Probably nothing pleases a golfer more than hitting a good drive. I feel it sets you up confidently for the rest of the hole and is probably the most important shot next to the putt. A good start and there is less tension on the successive fairway shots, so you will probably hit them well too!

The driver is the longest club in the bag and for the average player the most difficult to use. Its extra length gives more clubhead speed, which in conjunction with its low loft results in greater length potential. Any basic swing faults will be exaggerated, so you must set up your best stance and swing.

Because the club is the longest, you need to stand further from the ball and this increases the margin of error. Thinking about the following will help:

• Check your correct distance from the ball by dropping the driver against your front leg as explained in Chapter 2. This is most important because if you are too close, you will cramp the shot and probably slice it.

• The ball should be opposite your front heel (be careful it is not opposite the toe, a common, careless fault). It needs to be in this position so the ball is hit on the upswing to get maximum distance and roll from the low loft on the club.

• The height of the ball on the tee is also important. When using the driver, half the ball should be above the top of the clubface. Too high,

you may sky it; if too low, you will almost certainly top it as you hit on the upswing.

• Make certain body alignment is correct and square, and swing as explained in Chapter 3.

• It is particularly important to relax and not try to hit the ball too hard. This is a natural psychological desire which must be overcome. The top pros often look as though they are hitting the driver very hard — and they probably are — but it takes years of dedicated, constant practice to do it consistently and the average golfer shouldn't even try if he wants to score reasonably. Think instead of making a wide, free-flowing, relaxed swing.

Other woods off the tee

Many golfers (including some pros) drive with a 2 wood and find it easier because the shaft is slightly shorter and there is a little more loft. Perhaps try a driver with 11 or 12 degree loft. For the senior golfer, accuracy is all important, so if you are more confident with one of these, or even a 3, by all means use it. If you do, you may find it better to move the ball progressively closer to centre as the loft increases or you may end up expending much of your energy hitting the ball in a very high trajectory and therefore losing distance.

Above: *An easy way to check your set up and swing for the drive: ball correct height and opposite front heel; shoulders, hips, knees and feet square to the ball-to-target line.*

Left: *Halfway back in the swing, the weight is transferring to the back leg; the hips and shoulders are turning and the arms and club are still extended parallel to the target line.*

Above: *At the top of this full backswing, shoulders and hips have maximum pivot, weight on back foot, front arm slightly bent, wrists fully cocked. If you cannot pivot, stop your backswing anywhere between halfway and the full swing. You will lose some distance but may gain accuracy.*

Above right: *Halfway into the follow-through, head remains perfectly still, weight is entirely on front foot; arms and club are fully extended parallel to the ball-to-target line.*

Right: *Follow-through completed, body facing the target, all weight is on the front foot with just the toes of the back foot grounded to maintain good balance. Again, if you cannot turn to face the target, complete the follow-through at a point to match the end of the backswing.*

Playing woods off the tee is demonstrated here and on the next page: relaxed stance at address after a final look at the target to check alignment. Ball opposite front heel. At the beginning of the backswing, arms and clubs are taken straight back on the target line until the hip and shoulder pivot commences and weight transfers to back leg; the wrists are cocked. Note that only the toes of the front foot are on the ground at the top of the backswing.

A golfer with a restricted backswing can stop it at any point, provided the same swing plane is maintained.

When playing woods off the tee, during the downswing the head remains still and elbow brushes hip; hands ahead of clubhead at impact (see left).

On follow-through, back arm and club extend towards the target, with elbow straight until almost parallel to the ground. Weight is already almost entirely on front leg and head remains still until pivot forces it round to follow line of shot. Balance is perfect throughout swing and at completion, showing there has been smooth rhythm throughout the shot.

Again, the follow-through can be stopped to match the backswing — but maintain the same swing plane.

Irons off the tee

There is no reason why you shouldn't use long irons off the tee on a par 4 or even par 5 hole if you feel more confident with them, particularly onto a narrow fairway when accuracy is all important. A 2 or 3 iron can hit a long way, particularly in dry conditions.

Stand closer to the ball because the shafts are shorter and, as with the loftier woods, place the ball inside the front heel.

Tee the ball lower for irons, but you may need to have less than half the ball above the clubface to get the correct trajectory with some of the modern large-faced clubs. With a little experimentation, you will soon find the correct height.

The swing is the same as for the woods.

FAIRWAY SHOTS

Fairway woods

Whether you select a wood or an iron on the fairway will depend upon the lie and route to the target. The 3 wood is probably the most widely used. The 2 is tricky unless the ball is sitting up well on a lush fairway.

The 4 and 5 are also very useful weapons, particularly out of light rough, and are relatively easy to use with their shorter shafts and greater loft.

The same basic stance and swing apply as for the tee shot woods — and the stroke should be smooth, slow and *never forced*.

Study the lie and terrain ahead carefully before selecting a club. Don't give up on the short woods if you find them difficult to start with. With experience, they will produce some very enjoyable and accurate shots. In fact, some golfers find them easier to use than the long to medium irons. Even 6 and 7 woods are quite widely used these days and can provide salvation for some senior golfers fighting against stiff joints and muscles to maintain reasonable distance and accuracy!

My advice is to use whatever suits your style of game and physical characteristics best, and provides you with maximum enjoyment! I have a friend who, at the age of 62, plays to a regular 18 handicap on a difficult undulating course, but never puts a wood in his bag! You might say he'd soon be down to 12 if he did, but the point is he gets great enjoyment playing as he does! That's what it's all about.

Fairway irons

Long irons — 2, 3 and 4

I said that hitting a good drive is one of the most satisfying sensations in golf. For me, there is also a great satisfaction in hitting a 2 iron 210 yards (190 m) or so to the heart of the green. Certainly such a shot brings very appreciative applause and a kind of awe from the gallery in a tournament.

Many golfers find long irons difficult because they believe they have to swing differently to make them work. This is not so. The basic stance and swing is the same as for the woods. The only modifications you need to consider are caused by the shorter shafts and the need to hit down on the ball. These are:

• A slightly narrower stance.
• Standing closer to the ball.
• Placing the ball somewhere between the front heel and the centre of your stance.

The reason the ball is placed closer to the centre of your stance is so that you hit down and through the ball, taking a divot. This enables the loft of the club to impart backswing and lift the ball into a high trajectory. However, you use the same basic swing to do it. The different ball position enables you to hit down on the ball rather than the sweep produced by hitting the ball on the upswing when it is opposite the front heel and teed up.

I believe it is particularly important to make certain the takeaway is slow and deliberate. The whole swing only takes a few seconds — but the backswing must not be rushed and should always take longer than the downswing. I also concentrate very hard on staying on the same plane, in line with the target, swinging back and down. You use irons for accuracy and therefore it is very important to swing accurately and in line with the target.

This sequence shows a long iron shot. Note the same basic swing, but feet slightly closer together and ball closer to centre.

Checking alignment

The exercise used to check woods alignment and swing is applied here to a 4 iron played off the fairway.

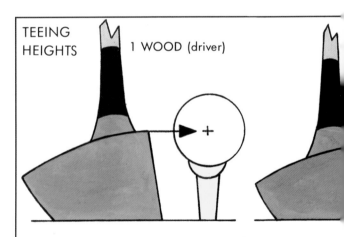

TEEING HEIGHTS   1 WOOD (driver)

Half the ball should be above the clubface when a tee peg is used, but take into account that the

The same basics are being demonstrated. Note in particular: the ball a little closer to centre; the chin held well clear of the chest allowing shoulders to turn freely; the knees moving towards the target just before impact with the elbow close to the hip; excellent balance with the hips and shoulders pivoting around the spine with no sideways sway.

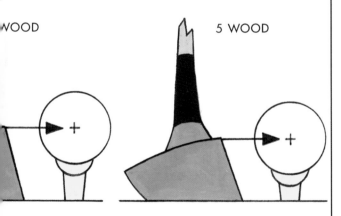

WOOD 5 WOOD

height of the clubface varies according to its loft. This applies to the long irons as well as to the woods.

Medium or middle irons — 5, 6 and 7

Most people find these clubs the easiest because the length of the shaft feels comfortable and the loft looks as though it will pick the ball up nicely.

The address and swing is exactly the same as for the long irons. To select the correct club, carefully examine the lie and route to the target. Weather, particularly wind, also has to be considered.

Playing off lush grass or short rough, blades of grass can get between the ball and clubface. This increases distance because it cuts out back spin and the ball tends to fly, so use a shorter club, e.g. come down from a 5 to a 6.

Really, there are no hard and fast rules; you just have to weigh up all the conditions and make your own decision. That is one of the fascinations of golf and why it is such a great leveller. One time you make the right choice, the next you don't, so be content to play the percentage game to minimise frustration and maximise your performance and enjoyment!

Checking a 9 iron address. The feet are closer together, knees more flexed and the ball closer to centre. Shorter backswing and follow-through if necessary.

Short irons — 8, 9, wedge, sand iron

These are mostly used to play the approach shots. With shorter shafts and more lofted faces, they are designed for accuracy rather than distance. They are the clubs which, more than any others, can put you close to the pin, putting for a birdie.

Because they are shorter, you will need to stand slightly nearer the ball (check the position of the club on your leg as explained in Chapter 2). But make sure you are not too close and cramp your shot (rotund players take special note!)

Except, perhaps, for a slightly shorter backswing, and standing closer to the ball when playing full shots, everything should be the same as for the longer irons. (Chipping is covered in Chapter 7.)

However, some players favour a slightly open stance, which allows more freedom for the knees and hips on the downswing and enables the club to travel freely through the shot towards the target. For a heavier or stiffer player, this may be a wise option, but make absolutely certain you stay on the line through both the backswing and downswing, and for as long as possible on the follow-through. I have seen people crouch over their short irons — don't! You may flex your knees a little more but don't let your torso and shoulders bend over the ball.

See that the ball lies slightly front of centre and concentrate on making your normal golf swing, paying particular attention to rhythm and balance. Remember, you want accuracy, not distance!

This is perhaps the most important department for the senior golfer. Because there is no demand for power and distance, the emphasis is very much on accuracy, control and feel. Many senior golfers I have played with have astonished me with their ability to hit like demons with these clubs. When I ask for the secret of their success, they simply reply 'lots of practice, and because I cannot reach the long par 4s in 2 shots, I must have a good short game to score reasonably well.'

THE SWING PLANES

To help understand the all-important swing plane, imagine your head at the centre of a dinner plate and your clubhead travelling up and back around its rim and therefore on a constant plane. The angle of this plane can vary according to the length of club but it must be constant for each club and link with the ball-to-target line.

1

2

3

4

5

6

Full short iron shot

This sequence 1-7 shows Bob Charles playing a full short iron shot. Stance, alignment and swing are all the same except that he has shortened his backswing a little and stands closer to the ball (to allow for the shorter club). Note in 5 how long into the follow-through his eyes remain on where the ball was, and how he has kept his head perfectly still.

7

Two senior golfers show how they do it

Setting up with a driver. Good relaxed stance with knees slightly flexed, though arms and hands look a little tense. Back foot is slightly splayed out to make backswing pivot easier. At the top of the backswing, there has been good shoulder turn, but the front arm should be straighter and the wrists have not cocked enough. Not enough weight has been transferred to the back leg. The lady golfer has these things almost right. A good finish to the follow-through with weight transferred to front leg.

Summary — swing sequence

Woods off the tee:
1. Check you are not too close to the ball.
2. Ball opposite front heel for driver; a little towards centre for loftier woods.
3. Check ball height on tee peg.
4. Square body alignment.
5. Visualize a sweeping, relaxed swing motion.

Irons off the tee:
1. Stand closer to the ball.
2. Tee ball lower.
3. Swing as for woods.

Fairway woods:
1. Number 3 woods and above are easier to use.
2. Swing and place ball as for woods off the tee, closer to centre if lie not too good.

Fairway irons, long to mid:
1. Narrower stance.
2. Stand closer to ball.
3. Depending on club loft, place ball between front heel and stance centre.
4. Swing down on the ball and be careful to stay on the same plane in line with target throughout swing.
5. Basic swing is the same.

Short irons, full shots
1. Stand slightly closer to the ball, but not too close to cramp swing.
2. Shorten backswing slightly.
3. You may prefer to open stance a little to allow more freedom for knees and hips, but be sure to stay on the correct swing plane and target line.
4. Concentrate on rhythm and feel.

Chapter 5

SWING DRILLS

Golf may not demand such a high standard of fitness as tennis, squash, rugby or soccer, but one must ask 'Do we play golf to get fit, or get fit to play golf?' As we get older, we take longer to loosen up, so here are a few simple exercises recommended by a teaching professional who specialises in helping *seasoned* players; they may help you.

You can practise swing drills anywhere, inside or outside, at any time. A good time is when you are waiting to take your place on the first tee, or if there is a hold-up in play; they can help you to keep your rhythm. And don't be self-conscious about doing swing drills in front of your playing partners; the chances are you will win the hole because you've kept moving. It's very likely that you'll be copied!

However, be careful not to distract nearby players making shots on adjacent fairways and greens — or even on your hole if they have strayed from the straight and narrow!

Swing drills

Above left: *Place the golf club through your elbows and across your lower back. Link your hands together in front. (Breathe in if you have to!)*

Above: *Rotate your body fully on the backswing until the clubhead would be pointing directly at the ball. Note how the front knee moves across towards the back knee and the front heel is raised slightly off the ground.*

Left: *On the follow-through, rotate your body until the grip of the club is pointing directly at the ball. Body weight will now be on the front leg with the back toes positioned like a ballerina and your belt buckle facing towards the target.*

Above: *Stand upright with the butt end of the grip against your belt. Hold the club down the shaft until your arms are reasonably straight. Keep your chin high.*

Above right: *Halfway back, note how the front knee has moved across towards the back knee and how the butt end of the grip has remained against the belt. The toe of the club is pointing upwards.*

Right: *Halfway through, the butt of the grip is still against the belt and the weight is entirely on the front side; the toe of the club is pointing upwards.*

Left: *Swinging two clubs together is a good exercise for the hands and arms; it also helps to develop good rhythm in the swing. Note: you may find it easier not to grip the two (or three) clubs as you would a single club. Instead, use a baseball or cricket bat grip with the thumb of the top hand on the outside; this will relieve pressure and strain. At the top of the backswing, the clubs are positioned above the back shoulder. At the completion of the follow-through the body is facing the target with the clubs above the front shoulder.*

Above right: *Place your outstretched front arm on the butt end of the grip and swing the back arm under the front arm. This keeps the back shoulder down under the chin. (Good exercise for slicers.)*

Right: *A down-the-line view. The lower body has transferred the body weight back onto the front side; the upper body remains back and down, under the chin.*

Left: *Preparing for the 'pure swing drill'. Hold the club at the top and bottom of the grip with the thumb and index finger. At the top of the backswing, note how the club is supported above the back shoulder and how the front knee has moved towards the back knee. At the end of the follow-through, the club is supported above the front shoulder and the weight is entirely on the outside of the front foot. This only works if your golf swing is correct, so it's a good test.*

The feet together drill. Place the clubhead opposite front foot and swing. If your swing is correct you should be able to retain your balance at the top of the backswing and follow-through. This exercise is very good for balance and the correct hand and wrist action. If you do something wrong, you will probably fall over!

Putting drills

Above: *Putting towards two golf tees is good practice as the target is very small. This means that when you turn your attention to the actual hole, it will seem like a bucket in comparison.*

Above right & right: *Putter under arms drill. This helps you concentrate on the pendulum action of arms and shoulders pivoting around the neck — this should be the only movement. On the backswing, the grip of the club finishes pointing diagonally to the ground. On the follow-through, the grip finishes pointing diagonally towards the sky. This completes the essential pendulum movement of shoulders and arms.*

Chapter 6

BUNKER SHOTS / SAND TRAPS

BUNKER shots are often among the most feared for the higher handicap player; in fact I've had more difficulty with them than with any other part of my game.

However, with the correct technique, bunker play can be relatively straightforward and perhaps even enjoyable! Apart from mastering the technique, which requires a lot of practice, there is a lot of psychology in the shot too. The key is to approach it with confidence.

Normal lie

First of all, a good sand iron is essential. This club, with its wide flanged sole and back edge lower than the leading edge, is designed to bounce off the sand under the golf ball without digging in too deeply, entering the sand approximately 2 inches (5 cm) behind the ball and exiting the

sand 4-6 inches (10-15 cm) after the ball.

If the sand is very wet or compacted, it is best to use a wedge or 9 iron as you need to cut under the ball; the sand wedge will bounce off the hard surface.

I stand with a very open stance and club face, with the ball opposite my front heel, particularly if plenty of loft is needed. Some players prefer not to open the stance and clubface so much and to have the ball nearer the centre. Again, it's an individual preference and both can work equally well. Whichever you use, the following points are important:

• Plant your feet firmly into the sand, fairly close together, no more than 18 inches (45 cm) apart. Wriggle them into the sand. This gives you a firm platform to hit from and enables you to feel the consistency and depth of the sand.

Above left: The feet, hips and shoulders are open to the ball-to-target line. Note that the clubhead is held above the sand as required in the Rules of Golf.

Above: The wrists have cocked early in the backswing to create the correct angle of attack on the downswing.

Left: The knees are moving towards the target and the clubhead has 'splashed' the ball out of the sand towards the hole. The head has remained still throughout the swing.

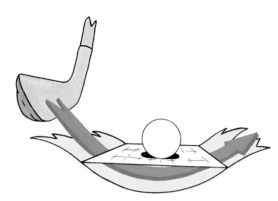

To get the feel of hitting under the ball and through the sand, place the ball on a score card and hit under it.

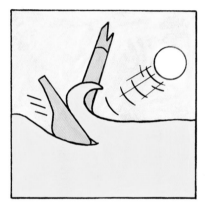

Hit underneath the ball and approx 2 inches (5 cm) behind it.

• Swing the club straight back relatively slowly from the ball in line with the target.

• Stop the backswing when your hands are somewhere between waist and shoulder height, depending on the distance the ball has to travel. Consequently there is not much hip turn; it is primarily an arm/shoulder action with the wrists cocking early.

• The downswing needs to be smooth and firm, the front arm and knee working together, pulling the clubhead down under the ball and accelerating towards the target. After impact, the clubhead should finish at approximately the same height as it was at the top of the backswing. On completion, the weight should be on the front foot, torso facing towards the target. You must be well-balanced with only the toes of the back foot on the sand. A well executed follow-through and balance are essential.

How do you control the length of your shot from a greenside bunker? There are basically two ways to do this. The first (and arguably the easiest) is to shorten your backswing and follow-through for a short shot, and make a longer backswing and matching follow-through for the longer shot. Using this method, you are still striking the sand about 2 inches (5 cm) behind the ball as normal. The second method is to swing the clubhead more steeply on the backswing so that more sand is removed from under the ball on the downswing; the swing is V-shaped rather than a flowing curve. This will make the ball travel a shorter distance than the normal swing.

When you want more distance, make a U-type swing, removing less sand from under the ball.

For more distance, I square my stance and the clubface which changes the swing plane. It still lofts the ball well but allows it to roll.

I recommend you experiment and practice to see which method suits you best.

Summary — normal lie

1. Always use a sand iron unless sand is very wet or hard-packed.
2. Wriggle feet into sand to get a firm stance.
3. Set clubface open at address; position ball anywhere from front of centre to off front heel.
4. Open stance and body alignment.
5. Strike sand approximately 2 inches (5 cm) behind ball.
6. Slowish, smooth backswing; firm downswing.
7. Follow-through matches the backswing, weight transferred to front foot. Finish well balanced.
8. The length of shot is governed by the length of swing or by opening or closing the stance.

1

2

3

4

5

6

Although Bob Charles tries hard to avoid bunkers, in common with all top tournament players he is a maestro at playing out of them. In this sequence 1-7 you see him at the start of the backswing, feet planted firmly in the sand about 18 inches (45 cm) apart, evenly balanced. At the top of the backswing, shoulders have turned but hip pivot is minimal. Head is still and eyes firmly on the ball. He is swinging smoothly and firmly into the impact area, the front arm and knee pulling the clubhead down to hit under the ball. Just after impact, the head remains perfectly still, the knees relaxed, back elbow close to the hip, and the ball blasts sharply up from the sand. Completing the follow-through, which as you can see is the same length as the backswing, the back arm is still straight, the weight has transferred onto the front foot; hips, chest and head have turned to face the target, and Bob is still perfectly balanced. The ball continues to rise steeply to the apex of its arc.

Finally, the arms relax as the ball pitches close to the pin!

7

Buried lie

The buried or plugged lie need not be as horrendous as it looks!

Position the ball in the centre of your stance. But don't stand open for this shot — stand parallel to your target line as in a normal shot. Close the clubface slightly by pushing your hands ahead of the ball — this creates a digging action. The wrists should cock early on your backswing to create a steeper angle of attack. Look at your strike point 2 inches (5 cm) behind the ball and drive the clubhead down into the sand. Don't expect much, if any, follow-through as your clubhead will tend to bury itself in the sand after impact. The ball will be popped out by the wall of sand your clubface has driven into it and come out very low, so allow for extra run.

When the ball is buried in the sand, close the clubface by pushing both hands towards your target.

Summary — buried lie

1. Close clubface by pushing hands ahead of ball.
2. Position ball in centre of stance.
3. Feet and shoulders parallel to ball-to-target line.
4. Strike sand 2 inches (5 cm) behind ball.
5. On backswing, break wrists earlier and drive clubhead onto strike point.
6. Allow for run.
7. Follow-through is unlikely as clubhead tends to bury itself in sand after impact.

Our senior golfers show what they can do in a greenside bunker. Both have used a slightly open stance in relation to the pin. Note clubhead above the sand in accordance with the Rules of Golf. The man is too hunched over the ball because he is not standing close enough to it.

The backswing is good with shoulder turn and little hip pivot; back elbow tucked in, though for both players the front arm could be straighter. Heads are still and eyes on the ball. There is very little wrist cock for this shallow bunker, so the ball will fly lower and run to the pin.

Good balance is maintained to the completion of the shot, weight transferred to front foot, with only the back toe in contact with the sand. The man is still too hunched but at least this shows he has maintained the same swing plane throughout the shot. It seems to have been an effective one judging from the position of the ball in flight. The woman's shot also looks as though it will finish very close to the pin.

From wet hard-packed sand

In this situation I recommend using a pitching wedge or a 9 iron rather than the sand iron; the soles of these clubs are narrower than a sand iron and will dig into the sand more effectively. The sand iron will bounce off hard, wet or muddy sand, and drive the ball straight into the bunker face, or worse still right through the green and over the out of bounds fence!

When playing from hard-packed sand, swing slightly more slowly than normal, giving the clubhead time to dig into the sand behind the ball, thus reducing the likelihood of a thin, skinny shot.

Playing from the fairway bunker

To play a long-distance shot from a fairway bunker you can use a 4 or 5 wood or long irons. Position the ball further forward than normal, opposite your front heel. Focus your eyes directly on top of the ball, then proceed to make your normal golf swing. Your aim is to strike the ball cleanly. Don't be too greedy for distance and always assess the height of the bunker lip and make sure you have enough loft to clear it.

Left: Bob Charles puts it all together again. Note plenty of wrist cock as this is a deep bunker and the ball must fly high; also his superb balance and follow-through, equalling the backswing.

Putting from a bunker

If a greenside bunker has a relatively shallow lip you may decide to 'putt' out of the sand. This is perfectly acceptable. I would recommend that you position the ball fairly far forward in your stance, as this will help you produce some top spin to keep it rolling towards the hole. Remember that the Rules of Golf forbid you to ground your putter in the hazard.

Summary

— *wet hard-packed sand*

1. Use a pitching wedge or 9 iron.
2. Swing more slowly to allow clubhead to dig well into sand behind the ball.

— *playing from fairway bunker*

1. Check lie of ball. Choose club with sufficient loft to clear lip of bunker.
2. If bunker lip low and distance is needed, use fairway wood or long iron.
3. Position ball further forward than normal. Focus eyes on top of ball.
4. Swing normally.

— *putting from bunker*

1. Be careful not to ground your club.
2. Position the ball fairly far forward.

Chapter 7

PITCHING AND CHIPPING

THIS aspect of the game need not be affected at all by any physical defects the senior golfer may have collected over the years! There is no demand for power and distance — the prime needs are accuracy, control and feel. Pitching and chipping can be done with very little movement of the waist and shoulders and can be practised easily as little space is required.

And, above all, it is a key stroke saver. You may not reach the green in one, two or three shots but if you are within 80 yards (75 m) or so, with plenty of practice you should be able to land the ball frequently within one-putt range of the pin, making up for your extra fairway shot.

There are a number of successful methods. Because it is relatively easy to practice, it is not difficult to decide which is best for you. Here are some of my thoughts on the subject.

The object is to pitch the ball onto the green to avoid the awkward bounces that often occur when it is pitched short or even onto the apron of the green.

From about 90 yards (80 m) out I use a sand wedge, but not if the fairway is rock hard, as the club's thick sole will cause it to bounce into the ball rather than slice under it. In that situation use an ordinary wedge, or you may even decide to risk the bad bounce and roll it towards the green with a less lofted club.

I use a wedge from 100 to 120 yards (90-110 m) out and sometimes close to the green. However, most of my pitching is done with a sand iron.

Pitch shot

This is how I suggest you set up for the pitch shot:

• Stand closer to the ball, but not too close to restrict arm and knee movement.
• Feet closer together, perhaps about 6-12 inches (15-30 cm) apart depending on your build.
• You may hold the club low down the grip to shorten the shot and improve control, but I don't.
• Position ball slightly front of centre.
• Keep backswing short with very little shoulder movement and the follow-through of equal length. Think of a pendulum; shorten the swing for short shots and lengthen it for longer ones.
• Knee movement is minimal but there must be enough to transfer weight and provide acceleration.
• Hands ahead of the ball at address and impact.
• Prevent the clubhead travelling faster and thus ahead of the hands; skinny shots will result if it does.
• To get a good mental image of the shot, imagine it as a miniature, slightly modified and slowed-down version of the full swing. Keep it smooth, hit the ball with an accelerating blow but don't force it; keep your head still and eyes on the ball where it was at impact until well into the follow-through.

*Left: A pitch and run shot from just off the green played with a sand wedge because the ground contour was not suitable for a putter or medium iron. Note that body rotation, weight transference and wrist cock are all **very** slight. The shot is made primarily with a pendulum action of arms and shoulders.*

Pitch and run

From 2 to 5 yards (2–4.5 m) out I take a wedge or 8 iron (unless I can putt). You may prefer a 9 or even a 6 or 7. The shot is played in much the same way as the full pitch, except that the backswing and follow-through are shorter to compensate for the shorter distance. Because there will be very little shoulder movement, it is important to keep knees and body relaxed, to prevent strain in the hands and arms which will be doing virtually all the work, apart from some weight transfer to the front foot.

You need to work out how far the ball will run after it has pitched. This will vary according to the condition of the putting surface but, as a general rule, a wedge or 9 will travel through the air for two-thirds of its total distance, and roll a third of its total distance. A 6 or 7 will be in the air for one-third and roll two-thirds of its journey.

Run shots with lofted clubs

If the ground contour allows I always use a 4 iron — if I can't use a putter — for the shots close around the green. I grip it and swing it as I do my putter; no wrist cock, no body rotation, no weight transfer, just the arms and shoulders move the club.

If you prefer a 5, 6 or 7 iron, that's fine. But once you have made your choice, stick with it. If you hit a bad patch, don't change the club, get out and practise with the original one!

Run shots with the putter

When the conditions are right, close to the green I always use a putter. Over the right surface, it is the safest club in the bag. I think the easiest way to tell you *when* to use it is to give you some examples of when not to use it:
• If the grain of the apron grass is against you.
• If the grass is too high.
• If there is too much apron to cross.
• If there are humps and mounds to negotiate.
• If the green is very fast.

In fact, it is not difficult to work out for yourself.

This pitch sequence, further out from the green, is being played with a wedge. There is a little more

body rotation and weight transference than for the shot played close to the green, but again the

arms and shoulders act like a pendulum. Note the hands ahead of the clubface at impact and the follow-through (above) is the same length as the backswing.

The high grass pitch and run

To find your ball cradled deep in thick, lush grass within a metre (yard) or two of the green is a worrying sight! But it need not be daunting, although I must confess that to get it up and onto the green reasonably close to the pin is not easy! This is how I tackle it:

• With a sand wedge, almost as though I was playing out of a bunker.

• Length of backswing and follow-through is dictated by distance.

• By hitting behind the ball so the thick flange under the clubface cuts through the grass under the ball. It then jumps up and onto the green and rolls towards the pin. I close the face a little which helps prevent the flange from bouncing the club into the ball with potentially disastrous results.

• Note: this is not a jab shot; the follow-through is essential to retain control over direction and distance.

Left: A chip played from the fringe of the green with a number 7 iron. No wrist action but pendulum motion result in the clubhead travelling low to the ground, producing a shot like a putt but lifting the ball over any uneven surface at the edge of the green.

Right: The pitch and run from thick grass close to the green is played here with a sand wedge. Hit behind the ball, cutting through the grass under it — a free flowing pendulum-type shot with virtually no knee movement or wrist cock.

Our senior lady plays a pitch shot over the bunker — a shot that need not frighten you, as she demonstrates! Select a club to give sufficient loft to clear the hazard (here it is a sand wedge) and then proceed as for any other pitch and run shot. The stance is slightly open, the ball to front of centre. The shot is played primarily with the shoulders and arms. However, in this case there has been a little too much knee and waist movement.

A well executed chip and run shot with a 7 iron. All movement is confined to the arms and shoulders, producing a pendulum action which finishes with the clubface following the ball towards the pin. The stance is a little too crouched because the ball should have been closer. However a good result, as can be seen from the two previous balls sitting close to the pin.

These are shots that many senior golfers play and score well with; they are not physically demanding and can be practised in very little space.

Chapter 8

PUTTING

PUTTING is regarded by many as the most important part of the game; hence the old saying, 'You drive for show and putt for dough!'

It has certainly won me a number of tournaments including the British Open in 1963, the Canadian Open in 1968, the World Match Play in London in 1969, the South African Open in 1973, the Senior British Open in 1989 and 1993 and over sixty tournaments around the world.

I have always thought the putting stroke to be the easiest of all. The only parts of the body that move are the hands, arms and the shoulders, and no physical strength is required. But simple though the technique is (and there are many variations to choose from) the one you choose must be practised and mastered if you are to win matches on the green.

The other vital aspect of good putting is the ability to read the greens, see the line and assess the speed necessary to reach the cup. Only experience and a lot of practice will make you competent in this skill.

The grip, stance and stroke

The grip is entirely personal. I use the reverse overlap with the index finger on the top hand overlapping the second two fingers on the bottom hand (a variation is for the index finger to overlap just the little finger). The hands being close together working as one unit creates more control and feel. Both my thumbs are on the top of the shaft pointing directly at the putter blade. The back of my top hand faces the line of the putt and the bottom of my back hand faces in exactly the opposite direction. This ensures my stance is square to the line — feet, hips and shoulders.

My eyes are directly above the ball which I position just inside my front heel, weight evenly

Different putting grips

Bob Charles (above and right) uses the reverse overlap with the index finger of the top hand overlapping the second two fingers on the bottom hand. Because the hands are close together, working as one unit, he finds control is easier.

The grip is very much a personal thing. Many golfers use their normal grip; more often than not, the overlapping Vardon method (left, see Chapter 1). Some, like our senior lady, extend the index finger of the bottom hand down the shaft towards the blade for greater control and feel. A few use the extended broom-handle type of club, with the top hand stationary at chest height and the bottom hand down the shaft at normal height, moving the whole club as a pendulum.

distributed on both feet.

I stroke the ball with a pendulum motion. There is no wrist cock — just the arms and shoulders produce the stroke. The follow-through should be at least as long as the backswing, which will be dictated by distance and conditions. The head must be still (but don't let that freeze your whole body) and do not look up until the follow-through is completed. A good tip for a short putt is not to look up until you hear the ball rattle into the cup!

Many successful players prefer to use their normal grip and I have seen all sorts of putting styles used to good effect. I believe that if you find a method that feels good (and tends to have good results) you should stick with it, even if it is reverse handed with the top hand below the bottom on the club. But I think you would be wise to apply the basics of my stance and putting swing to your preferred style.

Remember, that in order to become a good putter you will probably need to spend lots of time on the practice green developing the method you feel is best. One simple tip is to putt towards a golf tee from approximately a yard or metre away until you can hit the tee confidently most times. Then when you turn your attention back to the hole it will seem like a bucket in comparison!

Use your putter to check body alignment is square to the ball-to-target line — across chest, hips and in front of feet.

Lining up

As you approach the putting green, have a look at the general contours of the ground around it. This will help you establish the way your putt will borrow (break). Your ball will react in exactly the same way as water on a slope, and run downhill. When you have decided which way the ball is going to borrow, stand behind it and visualise a line running from it directly to the point of borrow or, if a straight putt, directly into the centre of the hole.

Most top putters stand with the ball at a point inside the front heel to ensure striking it fractionally on the upswing to create top spin and thus help it to roll consistently towards the hole.

The feet, knees and shoulders should be parallel to the ball-to-target line — the railway line principle (see Chapter 2); the body bent over from the waist so that the eyes are looking directly down onto the ball. This helps to create a clear image of the correct line you wish the ball to follow.

The actual swing is controlled by the arms and shoulders with hands merely acting as the link with the grip of the putter. Keep your head still.

Most good putters favour placing the ball inside the front heel to ensure striking it fractionally on the upswing to impart top spin. Bend over the ball from the waist so that the eyes are directly over the ball.

The pendulum-type swing is controlled by the arms and shoulders. There is no wrist cock and the head and knees are still.

Above left: *Looking down the line of the putt. The eyes are directly above the ball, which is aimed to the right to allow for the slight borrow of the green.*

Above: *There is no conscious wrist action on the backswing. Instead the arms and shoulders work in unison, keeping the putter head low to the ground. The head remains perfectly still.*

Left: *On the follow-through, there has again been no conscious wrist action. The putter head is following the ball directly to the hole.*

Above: *Looking square on, the elbows are fairly close to the body and the ball is inside the front heel. Head is over the ball with the eyes looking straight down on it.*

Above right: *At the end of the backswing, the elbows are still fairly close to the body and the putter head is travelling low to the ground. The head remains still. Note the long backswing for a long putt.*

Right: *At the completion of the stroke, the putter head has travelled the same distance each side of the ball, i.e. the pendulum. Again the player's head remains still throughout the swing but, as this is a long putt, then turns slightly to follow the line of the ball, but not before the completion of the follow-through.*

Judging the speed

Many golfers are so 'line conscious' that they pay insufficient attention to the speed of the putt, a serious mistake as the speed has a direct influence on the actual line of the putt.

If you find it hard to judge speed, try this tip. On your practice green place some balls about two yards (2 m) from the hole. Stand back and look at the hole from behind the ball to establish the line. When you are ready to putt, close your eyes and try to feel the distance that is required. This way, you will soon begin to sink more putts as your 'feel sense' will be more aware and you will be amazed at how much your judgement of speed has improved. This is particularly important for long putts; if your speed is correct, then the line will be fairly accurate too.

Reading the grain (or nap)

Face the hole with the sun behind you. Look at the grass between the ball and the hole. If the grass looks shiny, then the grain is with you and your putt will take off fast and the grain will have no effect on line.

Putting across the grain, there will be hardly any effect until the ball slows, when it will be pulled into the line of the grain.

If the grass is dull and dark, then the grain is against you and the ball will travel more slowly.

These days, an increasing number of greens are not just cut in parallel lines but across too. Reading the grain and assessing the effect it will have on your ball is consequently very difficult. My advice is not to worry about it because, in a longish putt, the crossways grains will cancel each other out. But in the immediate area of the hole, the grain is likely to be in one direction. It is easy to read which way by examining the grass at the very edge of the side of the cup you are aiming for. If your ball is trickling slowly, or 'dying' into the cup, this grain can effect it.

On the subject of 'dying' putts, I have very strong views. Many golfers say that if you don't putt up to the hole firmly, you will often be short and so there is less chance of sinking it. But I have watched so many firmly hit putts on the correct line, catch the rim, spin round the cup and not drop. However, a dying ball on the correct line will always drop. So, I am a gentle putter, trying to putt to the hole and not past it. Short putts I trickle in.

Slow greens

Try striking the ball halfway up; this imparts more top spin and keeps the ball rolling towards the hole. Also lengthen and speed up the stroke.

Fast greens

Shorten the stroke and slow it down, but be sure to accelerate and not decelerate the forward stroke.

Wet greens

On very wet greens, allow half as much borrow as on normal greens.

Windy conditions

Make one simple adjustment; stand with your feet wider apart to give you stability against the wind. Then allow for some extra borrow as the wind will tend to affect the ball as it is slowing down.

'Broom handle' putters

The basic techniques for putting are age-proof. However, some senior golfers are using the new 'broom handle' type of putter. This helps to eliminate the 'yips' by keeping the top hand completely still, with the other hand simply moving the putter pendulum-style back and through. Try one out — you may discover something about putting that makes life easier — but still head for the practice green.

Eyes right over the ball, which for many golfers is too close to centre of stance (but this is a personal choice). The elbows are set fairly close to the body; arms and wrists are firm after impact, the result of a good shoulders and arms only movement. The head has turned to follow the line of the putt, but has remained still throughout and long enough after impact to ensure the putt is on line. But on short putts, don't look, just listen for the ball to drop!

Summary — putting

1. Check ball-to-target line from behind ball. Visualise a path from ball to hole. Look for grain.
2. Square stance, parallel alignment of shoulders, hips, knees and toes, applying railway line principle.
3. Bend forward from waist until your eyes are directly above the ball. Flex knees slightly.
4. Position ball inside front heel.
5. Make smooth low pendulum-like swing with arms and shoulders and follow-through at least as long as backswing.
6. Keep head still until completion of follow-through.
8. Short putts: don't look up until you hear the ball dropping into the cup!

Chapter 9

DIFFICULT SHOTS

Ball above feet: The hands are lower down the grip, with the weight set slightly forward on the toes.

A slightly flatter swing than normal because of the sloping lie. Remember to aim to allow for the ball hooking.

SLOPING LIES

A GOLFER often has to play shots from uneven ground. Remember that although you may be making a slight adjustment to your body alignment and address position, you are still trying to produce the same golf swing as if you were standing on the flat.

The four most common situations which occur are:

1. Ball above your feet.
2. Ball below your feet.
3. Ball on an uphill lie.
4. Ball on a downhill lie.

Naturally, the golf ball will react differently in each case but if you develop an understanding of how its flight will be affected, you will be able to deal with the problem more effectively.

Ball above the feet

In this situation the ball will travel through the air with hook spin caused by the arc of your swing which will be considerably flatter due to the awkward set-up position. To allow for this, the clubhead and address body position should be aimed at an imaginary target to the *right of the real one by a right-hander and to the left by a left-hander.*

Place the ball in its normal position for the club selected, shorten your grip to compensate for the slope and stand further away than usual, with weight towards your toes. This helps to keep your balance — *good balance is essential.*

Having made these slight adjustments, you should swing with a flatter plane than normal to compensate for the elevation of the ball.

Ball below the feet

A difficult situation as there is a tendency for the ball to travel through the air with slice spin. This is caused by the slightly more upright swing, created by the player having to stand closer to the ball at address.

To allow for this, right-handers should aim the clubface at an imaginary target to the *left* of the real one, and left-handers to the *right*. Place the ball in its normal position for the club selected, stand closer to the ball, select a longer club and hold it at full length. Keep your weight more on the heels to stop any tendency to fall towards the ball — good balance is essential.

Many golfers find it very hard to restrain a desire to force the ball in these situations — but again, *a smooth swing with good balance is all that is necessary for a good result.*

Above left and right: *The body weight is slightly more on the heels at address. Aim to allow for a slice. The swing is more upright than normal when the ball is below the feet. Again the weight is set slightly on the heels throughout the entire swing.*

Opposite left: *Uphill lie. The ball is positioned further forward, nearer the higher foot. Set your shoulders parallel to the slope as this will enable the club to continue on up the hill after impact.*

Opposite right: *Downhill lie. Position the ball further back in the stance to avoid striking the ground before contacting the ball.*

Ball on an uphill lie

In this 'launching pad' situation the ball will tend to fly higher with less distance than normal, so use a less-lofted club than you would on level ground. Your spine should be tilted until it is at right angles to the slope of the ground and your shoulders parallel to the ground. Most of your weight will fall naturally onto your back foot, but be careful not to let the knee buckle. Your front knee will bend to compensate for the uphill slope. The object is to get the club arcing with the slope.

Play the ball forward. Proceed with your normal golf swing, except that you may shorten the backswing to stop any sway and open the stance a bit, but do not change the plane. To maintain the all-important smooth swing and balance on the slope, it may help to think about leading the downswing with the knees. But do remember what I said in Chapter 3: *if you need to focus on one movement to get everything going, then it is only a means to an end to get everything co-ordinated and working together.*

If you want to loft the ball, strike with your hands a little behind the blade. To keep it low, move them ahead of the blade.

Ball on the downhill lie

Many golfers consider this the most difficult of all the uneven lie shots. The most common fault is to strike the ground before the ball. To avoid this, position the ball further back in your stance — towards the higher foot. Set your spine at right angles to the slope with your shoulders parallel to the ground. Choose a club with more loft than the one you would use on level ground as these shots tend to roll more.

Aim the clubface well to the left of the target (right-handers) and to the right (left-handers) as the ball will tend to slice from this position.

Keep weight on the front foot, swinging smoothly to follow the ground contour on the downswing, allowing the loft of the club to get the ball into the air. Most important, keep your head steady — there is a marked tendency to lift the head on or just after impact from a downhill lie. Hit through the ball maintaining rhythm and balance and you will have played one of the game's most satisfying shots.

Always have a few practice swings before attempting shots from any sloping lie to get the feel of the contours and so you can adjust your stance to them.

Summary — sloping lies

Ball above feet
1. Aim to allow for hook.
2. Shorten grip.
3. Weight on toes.
4. Normal balanced swing with flatter swing plane.

Ball below feet
1. Aim to allow for slice.
2. Weight on heels.
3. Full length grip.
4. Good balance and smooth swing.

Uphill lie
1. Spine at right angles to the slope.
2. Shoulders parallel to the slope.
3. Weight on back foot.
4. Shorten backswing.
5. Less lofted club than usual (e.g., a 4 instead of a 5) as shot will fly higher and lose distance.
6. Ball closer to front foot.

Downhill lie
1. Spine at right angles to the slope.
2. Shoulders parallel to the slope.
3. Weight on front foot.
4. Keep head steady.
5. Aim to allow for a slice.
6. More lofted club than usual (e.g., a 5 instead of a 4) as the ball will fly more
7. Ball closer to back foot.
8. Maintain rhythm and balance.

Left: *This downhill lie sequence shows that at the beginning of the backswing and coming into the impact area, shoulders are parallel to the downhill slope and the body is at right angles to it. Note ball closer to back foot.*

Right: *On the uphill lie the body stays at right angles to the slope throughout the stroke. At address and impact, shoulders are parallel to the slope.*

SHOTS FROM THE ROUGH

Deep rough

All golfers end up in the long, thick grass from time to time. When you do, forget about distance and concentrate on getting the ball to a better position for an approach to the green. Use a more lofted iron. Even then, there is a problem — if the heel of the iron strikes the thick grass or ground first, it can cause the face to close and the ball to be driven deeper into the grass.

I take a sand wedge, open the club face and cut through the grass under the ball, similar to a bunker shot, making sure I have a very firm grip to stop the club face turning. It does not matter if the grass prevents any follow-through; but try to keep an even pace to the back and downswing as you would from a bunker. With lots of practice you will soon become familiar and proficient with this shot.

In deep rough like this, the object is to cut through the grass under the ball. A sand wedge is being used to do this. The clubface is open and the club gripped tightly, low down, to prevent the face turning on impact with the grass. The backswing is at a steep angle, the clubhead has been driven down behind the ball and through the grass, which has prevented any follow-through. Look closely and you can see the ball has risen sharply and is on the way to the fairway.

Short rough

When playing from short rough, instead of using an iron club (which will tend to tangle up with even short but thick grass) try a 5 or 7 wood. Their rounded shape enables them to slice through the thick grass and the long shaft produces greater clubhead speed without extra effort.

Play the shot as though from a fairway but take into account that the ball will not fly as high and consequently will roll further.

It's more difficult if you are too close to the green for a wood. But the principle is the same if the distance dictates that you need, say, a 6 or 7 iron — but remember the ball will roll further.

If you are within 50 or 60 yards (45-55 m) of the green then my advice is to use a 9 iron rather than a wedge. Problem is that you often can't see the nature of the ground under the ball. The wedge has a heavy flange which may bounce off any hard ground, or even tightly packed grass, and crown the ball. The 9 iron has a sharper leading edge which is less likely to be deflected and so can be used more consistently.

Summary

—Deep rough

1. Open clubface as for a bunker shot.
2. On backswing lift club sharply.
3. Drive clubhead down onto back of ball and slice as far through the grass under it as possible.
4. Grip club firmly to prevent club face turning.

—Short rough

1. If distance sufficient, use a 5 or 7 wood, play normal shot but allow for longer run.
2. Close to green, use a 9 iron for easier control.

Low shots under trees

Many golf courses have trees bordering their fairways. Whilst this may be very attractive visually, it can prove to be most frustrating if your ball continually ends up in or behind them. So what we need is an easy method of extricating ourselves from these troublesome trees.

Do not automatically reach for your 2, 3 or 4 iron. Instead choose your 5 or 6 iron and proceed as follows: Position the ball well back in your stance, opposite your back heel. Push your hands ahead of the ball; this will close the face and de-loft your 5 or 6 iron and turn it into a 3 or 4, but you will still have the advantage of a club with a shorter shaft which will be easier to control.

In order to create tension in your hand and arms, grip the club tightly. This will restrict the length of your backswing and follow-through, usually the last thing you require in the trees! Little or no wrist cock.

During the backswing, make sure your front knee moves inwards towards your back knee; then on the downswing drive both knees towards your target. This will ensure that the clubhead strikes the ball cleanly and remains close to the ground after impact, avoiding striking overhanging branches and damaging the shaft.

The ball should fly under any branches and come out of the trees with lots of top spin, producing a running shot which will gain considerable distance.

Summary — low shots under trees

1. Use 5 or 6 iron; close face (gives a 4-iron loft with shorter shaft and easier to control).
2. Position ball further back, opposite back heel.
3. Grip club tightly to reduce length of backswing and follow-through.
4. Little or no wrist cock.
5. On downswing, drive knees strongly towards target. This gives clean contact with ball and keeps clubhead low to the ground, avoiding breakage and branches.
6. Allow for run as ball will emerge with top spin.

Using a 5 or 6 iron to hit under a low branch. Ball is opposite back heel. Note the short backswing. This is achieved by gripping the club very tightly at address.

On the downswing, drive the knees towards your target. This ensures good contact with the ball and helps to keep the clubhead travelling low to the ground. Push hands ahead of the ball.

Shots very close to and on the wrong side of tree trunks (or other immovable objects)

Seemingly impossible shots can often be played with a little lateral thought and ingenuity. One of the most common is to find your ball has come to rest within 6 inches (15 cm) or so of a tree trunk, and on the side which makes it impossible for you to swing normally.

There are three possible solutions: declare the ball unplayable and drop out for a penalty; or, if there is a reasonable route back to the fairway which could enable you to achieve a better position than if you had dropped out, try one of the two plays illustrated on this page and described in the captions. You will be surprised how effective they can be — but they do need to be practised!

With back to target, hold the club at the bottom of grip. Swing the clubhead forwards and then backwards; the ball will travel fairly well with almost no effort whatsoever. Make sure you don't strike your ankle!

For the more ambitious player turn the club around onto its toe end and proceed to play the shot left-handed if you are right-handed and vice versa. This may require a little practice.

Deliberate hooks and draws, slices and fades

At some stage you will need to deliberately hook or slice the golf ball around an obstacle (probably a tree) situated directly in line to your target. This may appear daunting, but it is a relatively simple task which can be tackled by changing the alignment of your stance. It is not necessary to alter your grip in any way. It is difficult enough to perfect your grip for straight shots so do not be tempted to tamper with it for these shots.

Hook or draw

Aim the clubface and align your body and feet in the direction you want the ball to start flying to avoid the obstruction. The effect will be to close your shoulders, feet and hips in relation to the ball-to-target line. You must now swing the club from inside the line before impact to outside line after impact, to impart the draw swing on the ball. A flatter swing plane will help you achieve this in-to-out swing. Also, it helps if you position the ball more towards the front foot and try to swing the clubhead ahead of the hands at impact. The result will be an 'early' hit with the clubface closed slightly with the forward ball position. This produces the necessary spin on the

ball, sending it out around the obstruction.

The controlled hook is very much a 'feel' shot with the hands and needs a lot of practice.

Remember that when the golf ball has hook spin on it, it will travel further than normal, so you may need to select a club with more loft to allow for this.

Slice or fade

Aim the clubface and align your body and feet in the direction you want the ball to start flying to avoid the obstruction. The effect will be to open your shoulders, feet and hips in relation to the ball-to-target line. You must now swing the club from outside the line, before impact, to inside the line after impact, to impart the fade spin on the ball. An upright swing plane will help you achieve this out-to-in swing. It also helps if you position the ball more towards the centre of the stance. This produces the necessary spin on the ball, sending it out and around the obstruction.

Like the draw, the controlled fade is very much a 'feel' shot with the hands and needs a lot of practice.

Remember that when the golf ball has slice spin on it, it will not go so far, so you will need a club with less loft to travel the required distance.

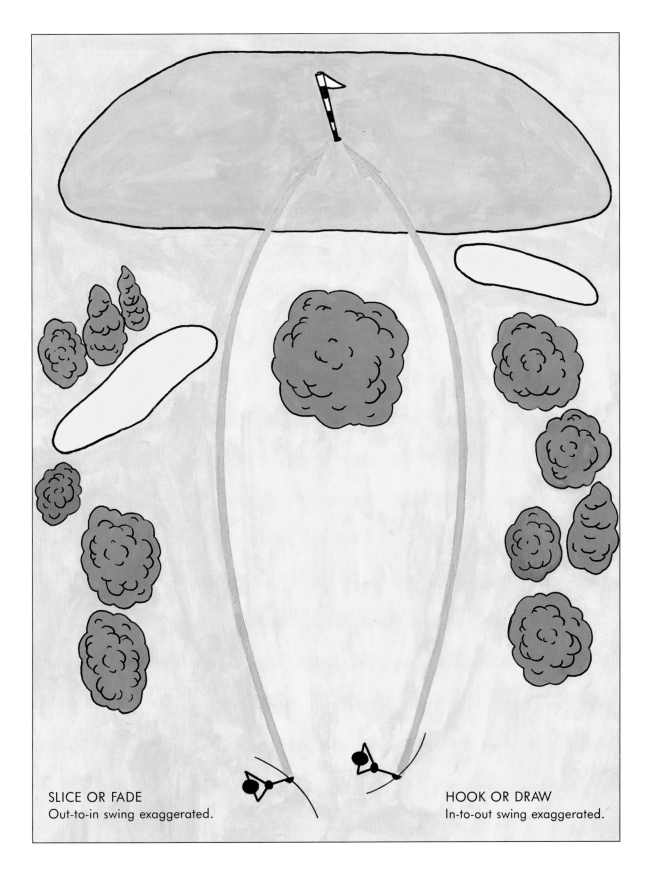

SLICE OR FADE
Out-to-in swing exaggerated.

HOOK OR DRAW
In-to-out swing exaggerated.

Chapter 10

FAULTS

THERE is a school of thought which says you should *not* correct faults but instead go back to basics and take up the correct grip, stance, swing and so on. In other words, thinking about what you are doing wrong introduces a negative element; that it is better to be positive by ignoring the bad shot and concentrate on playing the next one from the correct basics.

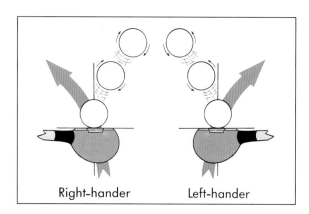

Right-hander   Left-hander

I am sure there is a lot of truth in that. But human nature being what it is, some people find it helpful to analyse their faults in order to get back to correct basics and it does help to understand and analyse the golf swing for those who like to do so. It also provides an opportunity for a refresher course.

So, here are a few common faults and their most common causes. For their cures refer to the appropriate chapter for the correct way of playing the shot.

Slicing

This is probably the most common fault in golf for the average player and has a number of causes.
1. *Open clubface at impact.* This happens if the hands are in a weak position on the grip of the club when the 'Vs' would be pointing at the front shoulder in the address position instead of the back.

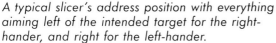

A typical slicer's address position with everything aiming left of the intended target for the right-hander, and right for the left-hander.

2. *Open body alignment.* The body is pointing to the left side of the target (right-handers) and right side (left-handers) but the follow-through is towards the centre of the target. This creates an 'out-to-in' swing path as the clubhead is pulled across the target line, leaving the clubface open at impact and imparting slice spin on the ball.

3. *Gripping too tightly.* This inhibits hand and wrist action and creates tension in the arms and shoulders, which results in upper body dominance and lack of weight transference. The result — slice spin on the ball.

4. *Weight on back foot at impact.* Check head position and balance in swing. Remember, swing back — weight on back foot; swing forward — weight on front foot.

5. *Hitting late.* Clubhead too far behind hands at impact.

Hooking

This shot probably affects good players more than below-average players. The causes are exactly opposite to those of slicing.

1. *Closed clubface at impact.* This can be caused by your hands being set too strongly on the grip as they would be if both 'Vs' are pointing past the back shoulder. This strong or hooker's grip always turns the clubface to the ball in a closed or shut position.

2. *Closed body alignment.* The body is lined up to the right side of the target (right-handers) and left side (left-handers), causing an excessive 'in-to-out' swing path with a closed clubface. This results in hook spin.

3. *Hitting early.* Clubhead too far ahead of hands at impact.

A typical hooker's address position with everything aimed to the right of the target for the right-hander, to the left for the left-hander.

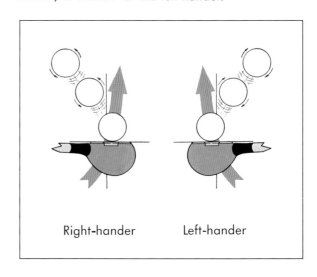

Right-hander   Left-hander

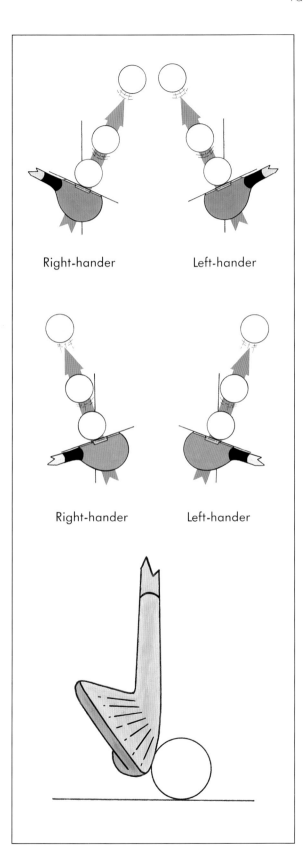

Right-hander   Left-hander

Right-hander   Left-hander

Push

This shot belongs to the 'in-to-out' family, the only difference being that the clubface is open at impact. A push shot has a higher than normal trajectory. There are two main reasons.
1. *Ball set too far back in the stance.*
2. *Late hit.*

Pull

This shot belongs to the 'out-to-in' family and the only real difference between the pull and the slice is the clubface position at impact. For the pulled shot it is square and for the sliced shot it is open.

There are two reasons for the pulled shot.
1. *Ball set too far forward.*
2. *Shoulders dominate the downswing.* This causes an 'out-to-in' swing path prior to impact.

Topping

The reasons for this are:
1. *Head and chin down.* Many golfers make the mistake of keeping the head down rather than steady. In fact, the chin needs to be up (though the eyes must be on the ball) to allow the shoulders to turn freely throughout the swing. Failure to do so can lead to a cramped shot which either tops the ball or even misses it completely.
2. *Weight transfer.* Failure to transfer the weight onto the front side during the downswing results in too much weight on the back foot at impact causing the blade to strike the ball on the upswing, so topping it.
3. *Ball too far forward of front heel at address.*

Fluffing or duffing

This is a fairly common fault, especially in women's golf. It is frustrating as it robs the player of distance because the clubhead strikes the ground before the ball.

The reasons for this are:

1. *Ball too far forward in stance.*
2. *Swinging up on the ball in an attempt to get the ball up.* Remember, to make the ball rise it must be hit on the descending swing arc not the ascending arc, except when teed up.
3. *Clubhead picked up too quickly.* If the clubhead is not extended back at the beginning of the backswing, the result will be a steep angle on the downswing causing the clubhead to strike the ground before the ball.
4. *Failure to transfer the body weight onto the left side during the downswing.*

Skying

This is another frustrating shot which only means loss of distance but can also damage the finish on your clubhead. Again there are several reasons.

1. *Failure to transfer weight onto the front side during the downswing.*
2. *Angle of swing too steep.* There has been a chopping or digging swing rather than a sweeping action.
3. *Hitting on the upswing.* A failure to transfer weight onto the front side on the follow-through.
4. *Teeing the ball too high.*

Socketing or shanking

One of golf's most dreaded shots which affects the mental as well as the physical side of your game. The ball slices off low at about 45 degrees to the target.

The causes are:

1. *Incorrect stance at address.*
2. *Clubface not square to target line on backswing or downswing.*
3. *'In-to-out' swing.* Players often assume an- 'out-to-in' swing is the problem, whereas the opposite is the main cause.

4. *Rolling the wrists too much.* This flattens the swing and can result in the shank or socket hitting the ball instead of the square clubface.
5. *Weight on toes or bad balance with head moving towards the ball, changing the swing plane.*

Fluffing or duffing

Skying

Socketing or shanking

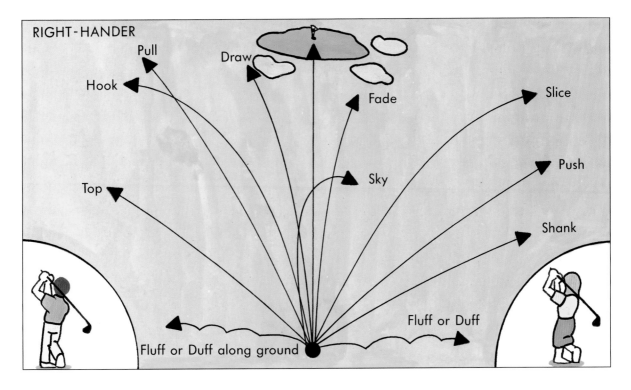

The common terms used to describe the direction of a shot. The straight, fade and draw shots are deliberate. The rest, with the exception of controlled hooks and slices round obstacles, are bad shots!

Top sketch for right-handers, bottom for left-handers.

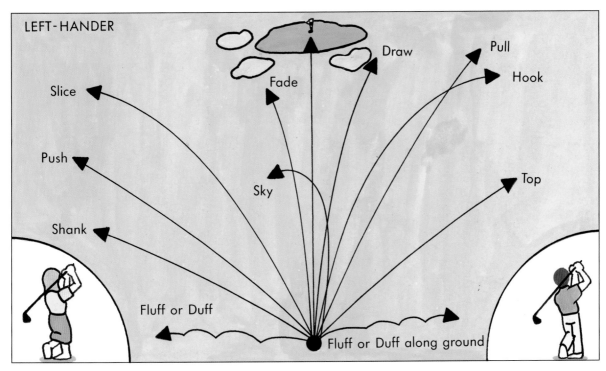

Chapter 11

PERCENTAGE SHOTS, TACTICS AND THE MENTAL GAME, PRACTICE, THE TEACHING PROFESSIONAL

TACTICS AND THE PERCENTAGE SHOT

MANY golfers fail to plan their tactics and play the 'percentage' shots. This is where seasoned golfers, wise in years, can outwit their more agile opponents and the golf course, by thinking about their game.

How often, for example, do you see players lofting the ball from just off the putting surface when there is no obstacle to play over? The shot should be played with a less-lofted club, perhaps with a putter, which will keep the ball travelling low to the ground. This would be playing the percentage shot as there is less likelihood of a mis-hit. And, it is an easier shot to play consistently.

When playing an approach shot to a heavily-bunkered green and the pin is tucked tightly just over the hazard, do not always play for the flag — consider aiming for the wide, safe part of the green. This will ensure that you at least have a *chance* of making your par. Again, this would be playing the percentage shot.

If there is a certain hole on your course which always seems to cause you some anguish, perhaps you need to change tactics. For example, a narrow tree-lined fairway with out-of-bounds running all the way down the right-hand side from the tee will generally require some careful planning if you are to avoid skirting with the out-of-bounds fence. Some players may opt to use a long iron or number 3 wood for safety; others may risk everything and go out with all guns blazing by using their driver. When you have decided which club to use, I suggest you try the following procedure.

First, on the actual teeing ground, make sure that you tee your ball up on the 'trouble' side (i.e. the right side in this case). Now you have the feeling of playing away from the out-of-bounds fence towards the safer part of the fairway. Let's assume you have chosen a long iron for the task; even if you 'overcook' it and it does go slightly too far left, the chances are that because you are playing a club that won't send the ball too far, the ball may well not reach the dreaded trees on the left-hand side of the fairway.

If your normal club selection (assuming that each shot has been hit correctly) is a number 1 wood followed by a 7 iron to the green, you might play instead a 3 iron from the tee, then another 3 iron which should almost get you on the green. Arguably, it should be slightly easier to hit two straight 3 iron shots than run the risk of spraying your driver and ending up with a double bogey or, worse still, losing your new ball over the out-of-bounds fence!

Remember, too, that when you are playing on a course with tree-lined fairways the sheltering trees may disguise wind movement. Always look up at the highest branches around you and take note of just how much they are moving, and in which direction. This will help you to allow for the effect of the wind on your ball which will probably be flying above the tree line and will be diverted to the left or right as it loses momentum.

Generally speaking, if you change your tactics slightly on the hole (or holes) that cause you problems, you will soon be making the occasional par again. This will have a tremendous positive effect on your confidence, and who knows, you may well start to actually enjoy playing that hole once more.

When playing on an unfamiliar course, take along a score card from your own club course, and when faced with a club selection, simply refer to your 'own' score card for a similar distance on your home course. This gives an indication of which club to choose on the strange new golf course.

If you find yourself having to go around a tree situated directly on your route to the target, apply the basic formula mentioned in the Deliberate

Hooks and Slices section in Chapter 9. It is safer than trying to loft the ball over the tree, and will get you greater distance. Even if the worst happens and your ball gets stuck in the branches of the tree, it's not the end of the world — you can always repeat the actions of Bernhard Langer, the top European player, who successfully extricated himself and his ball from the branches of a tree during the Benson and Hedges Open! There is a special plaque to mark this unusual and talked-about shot at the Fulford course in York, England.

The Mental Game

I believe that in order to play this great game at a reasonably proficient level you require a strong positive mental attitude as well as a sound swing.

How often do you hear golfers saying 'I knew my ball was going to end up in that lake', or 'I can't possibly play that shot.' This kind of negative thinking nearly always has an adverse effect on the shot you are about to play.

Visualise the shot. One of the best ways to improve your mental attitude is to visualise the kind of shot you want to play, then relax and let it happen. Naturally, if you have some basic swing errors, no amount of visualising or positive thinking will compensate for this fully, but it will certainly help your concentration level which must be functioning properly in order to play consistently good golf.

Most top tournament players would agree that visualising the result of a shot before you play it creates a clear positive picture of what you are trying to achieve. When you step up to play the shot, you expect the ball to behave exactly as it has in your mind already.

Positive thinking. Another way to improve the mental side of your game is to indulge in some positive thinking. Tell yourself how well you are swinging today, make bold statements like 'This lake no longer worries me', or 'I don't see how I can possibly miss this short putt.' It's amazing how much your golf game can be improved, by thinking clearly and positively. Your playing partners will be astounded at the sudden change in your game. They won't necessarily see any significant changes in your golf swing but will wonder as to the key of your new-found success. Just tell them that you have been working on a 'positive mental attitude'. With a good sound swing and the power of positive thinking, there is no limit to what you can achieve.

Pre-shot routine. I also believe it is very important to have a pre-shot routine that you follow before you hit every golf shot. Watch any of the great players — they all have a particular routine they go through whether just practising or playing the last hole in a major championship. This pre-shot routine should never vary as it will become an important part of your golf swing. The more comfortable and relaxed you feel at address, the better the chances of producing a super shot. And, of course, the more good shots you play, the more confident you will become in every department of your game.

Use both sides of the brain. It is now widely accepted that golf, like most other sports, should be played using both hemispheres of the brain; the left side (the 'analyser' side) controls the decision-making, e.g., 'I'll use a number 7 iron, aim slightly left to allow for the wind, and hit the shot high with plenty of spin'; the right side (the 'creative' side) visualises the flight of the ball and gives you the confident swing you require to land the ball close to the pin. If one side is working well and the other isn't, it would be the mental equivalent of playing with *half* a set of golf clubs! In other words, both sides have to be working in unison to create a well-balanced, clear-thinking, positive, confident golfer.

Bad golf shots are often the result of negative thinking and not, as ninety-nine percent of golfers believe, due to major swing errors. Some players are 'analysing' when they should be 'creating', and others 'creating' when they should be 'analysing'. Of course, some golfers are doing neither!

So as an exercise — say for a month — tell yourself every day how good a golfer you now are; try to think positively on every shot you play;

don't dwell mentally on the bad shots you hit, simply forget them, but do remember and think about all the good ones. You will soon find that by thinking confidently and positively your golf will improve out of sight.

Practice and Your Professional

It really does not matter what age you are — young or seasoned — if you want to play to the best of your ability and consequently gain maximum enjoyment from the game, getting the basics right and practising them is essential.

Get the basics right. The best way to do this is to go to a teaching professional. These days there are plenty around and you'll find them at the growing number of golf driving ranges as well as at your local golf club. Some people are shy about going to a pro. Others think they can learn it all from a book like this or from well-meaning friends. My advice is that you can't. You have got to have an expert look at what you are doing, tell you what is wrong and then show you a way to do it that suits your physical make-up. Even the top tournament players constantly seek advice from their teaching professionals.

So, if you are starting the game or want to improve, go to a pro. And I suggest you don't go along and ask for your slice to be fixed. Instead say 'I've started slicing a lot, must be something wrong with my basic swing or stance — can you put me on the right path again?' That way you will get the best out of your pro and the best value for your money.

Practise what you are taught. I also believe it is very important to practise what you are taught so that you are thoroughly familiar with it before you step onto the first tee to play a round. Of course, I realise that for many people time is limited so that a half hour or hour on the practice tee a couple of times a week is not always possible. But it is amazing how much you can do in and around the house, and even in the office!

At home. For example, take a few minutes daily to grip and re-grip a club; get the feel of it on a regular basis so it seems natural when you get on

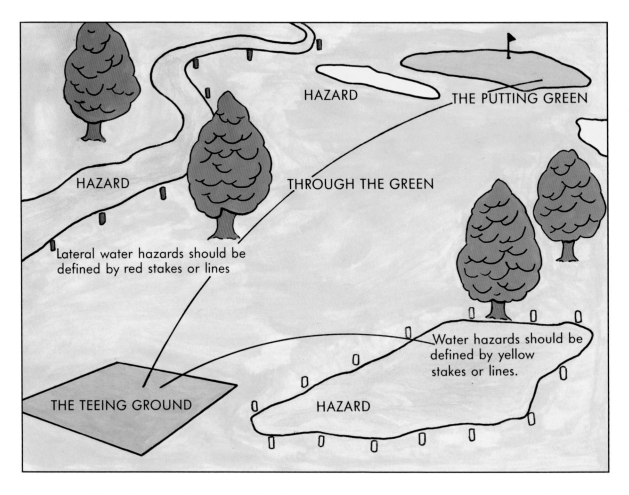

HAZARD

THE PUTTING GREEN

HAZARD

THROUGH THE GREEN

Lateral water hazards should be
defined by red stakes or lines

Water hazards should be
defined by yellow
stakes or lines.

THE TEEING GROUND

HAZARD

the course. There is no need to swing the club fully — a few wriggles are enough. If you have a garden or a room big enough to swing fully in, then do that too.

I find it invaluable to swing in front of a mirror, particularly to make certain my head is steady throughout the swing.

Refer back to Chapter 5 on swing drills — you can practise them all (or most of them) at home. Not only are they designed to help groove your swing correctly, but they exercise the muscles and joints we use in golf and help to keep them in good working order between rounds, a very necessary aid to enjoyable golf as we get older.

The practice tee or driving range. If you go to the practice tee or driving range, have a fixed programme in mind. Do not just hit a bucketful of balls as the fancy takes you. Work on a specific

problem until you have overcome it. If you can't, do see the pro.

For lessons to be really effective you need several over a month or more. Three or four day crash courses are also very valuable; they are organised by knowledgeable teaching pros in many parts of the world.

For a thorough workout go through the clubs from short to long irons and onto the woods. And don't forget the wedge and pitch and run shots. It is very important not to tire yourself or that will produce faults of its own! Remember, you will be hitting a lot of balls in far quicker succession than you would during a round. Take your time, think about each shot, and don't forget to work on controlled hooks, slices and other special shots for difficult conditions. Above all, work on building confidence in your ability to hit the ball and where you want it to go.

Chapter 12

EQUIPMENT

CLUBS

FIRSTLY, I would always recommend you seek the advice of your nearest qualified golf professional when it comes to choosing the right equipment for you. He or she will know which type of clubs suit your build and physique, especially if he or she has given you your initial golf lessons.

Most professionals carry an extensive range of new and used clubs so all you have to decide is how much money you are prepared to spend to begin with.

Remember that golf clubs always have a trade-in value, so there is no problem about 'trading up' to a full set of either new or used clubs at any time.

Many professionals have the facility to offer 'custom-made' half or full sets of clubs, so if you are extremely tall or very small, the length and weight of the clubs can be tailor-made to suit your requirements. A number of professionals are part of the 'golf connection' system whereby the customer's requirements are fed into a computer which advises what length of club they require, and what shaft flex, weight, grip thickness and lie of golf club they should use. This is an ideal method of taking the guesswork out of purchasing clubs.

The question of shoes, golf bag, trundler, glove, rain gear and golf balls can also be discussed with your professional, but I will mention some of these here.

Possibly the four main points to consider when buying golf clubs are:
1. That the 'lie' of the club is correct when assuming the correct posture at address.
2. The correct shaft flex.

3. The correct grip thickness.

4. Clubs correctly swing-weighted to your swing and physique.

Qualified golf professionals will always be happy to offer advice on these points.

Choosing the correct shaft flex

Golf shafts are made with different flexes, from very whippy to very stiff, and naturally this has an important bearing on the playing characteristics of any particular club. A young, strong, male golfer would certainly hit the ball further with ladies' flexible shafts but his direction would be very erratic indeed. On the other hand, the elderly lady golfer using 'stiff shafts' would hit the ball very straight but would be unable to generate any clubhead speed which creates distance.

The five most common shaft flexes fitted by manufacturers today are:

1. (L) Ladies.

2. (A) Active shafts, suitable for elderly men or strong women.

3. (R) Regular flex, suitable for the average male golfer or strong low-handicap woman.

4. (S) Stiff flex, suitable for the strong low-handicap male golfer, and often used by top tournament players.

5. (X) For the very strong tournament player.

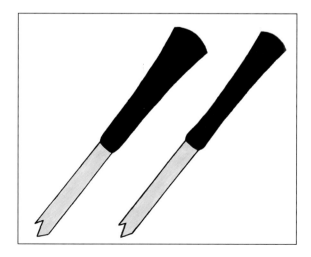

Grip too thick results in slice. Grip too thin results in hook.

Clubs for seniors

Over the last few years, the many changes and advances in golf equipment have created 'midsize' metal-headed clubs with graphite shafts, titanium shafts, etc.

Some manufacturers are now producing 'oversize' irons with much bigger heads. All of this means that, with the help of technology, today's golfer can find a set of clubs which hit the ball almost as far (and in some cases further) than they did in their younger playing days!

Discuss with your local professional the type that would most suit your game (and pocket!). Most pros have 'demo' sets available with various shaft options — graphite, titanium, steel and, in certain cases 'seniors flex' high torque graphite! Go on, try some out — I'm sure you'll love them!

Grip thickness

This very important aspect of the golf club should never be overlooked. If the grip if too thick or too thin you will be unable to grip the club correctly.

So when choosing your clubs, make sure the grips are the right thickness for you.

Grips for seniors

Many senior golfers have to change their grip slightly due to arthritis or some similar ailment as they advance in their golfing years. One of the most common changes is to have slightly thicker (jumbo) grips fitted. This helps the hands fit around the club and, because the grip is thicker, reduces the hand and wrist action, putting slightly more emphasis on the correct body action.

Consequently, if the golfer suffers from a restricted body pivot, then thinner grips can be fitted, thus putting more emphasis on the hand and wrist action, as the club nestles more in the fingers of the hand.

This would be particularly beneficial if the golfer's hands were unable to open fully due to arthritis or a similar condition.

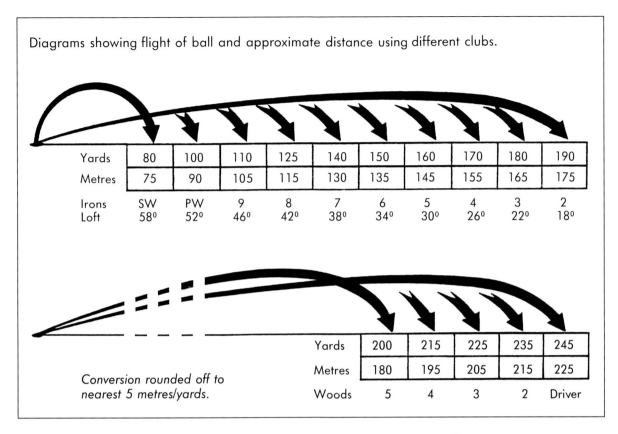

Diagrams showing flight of ball and approximate distance using different clubs.

Yards	80	100	110	125	140	150	160	170	180	190
Metres	75	90	105	115	130	135	145	155	165	175

Irons	SW	PW	9	8	7	6	5	4	3	2
Loft	58º	52º	46º	42º	38º	34º	30º	26º	22º	18º

Yards	200	215	225	235	245
Metres	180	195	205	215	225
Woods	5	4	3	2	Driver

Conversion rounded off to nearest 5 metres/yards.

Diagram showing the approximate distances the average male golfer can achieve using different clubs. Lady golfers and some seasoned golfers may hit shorter distances.

Wooden or metal woods

Another question I am often asked is 'Should I use a wooden wood or a metal wood?' My advice is to choose the metal-headed club, for four reasons: they are slightly cheaper to buy; they tend to hit the ball straighter; they require virtually no maintenance; and because the tend to become dry and shiny, and this may prove fairly expensive if you play golf regularly. Some players prefer the synthetic 'all-weather' glove which is ideally suited to wet conditions as the modern golf ball is so much 'harder', the metal heads stand up to the constant striking very much better than wooden ones.

Pros and cons of a golf glove

A golf glove gives much more 'feel', especially if it is in good condition. After a lot of use, gloves wetter it gets, the better the grip becomes.

If you decide to start playing golf without a glove, your hands will become tougher and you will probably never need one to improve your grip on the club.

A simple tip for drying out a wet leather glove is to place it between the pages of a glossy magazine. It will dry out slowly and avoid becoming hard and shiny.

Choice of golf ball

The most important points to consider are: the compression (see over), the durability, and how it feels at impact. Every golfer should look for these three qualities when choosing the ball.

There are basically two main balls available today: the solid or hard-centred ball covered with a thicker, tougher and cut-resistant cover made from man-made materials; and the softer wound ball covered by a thinner material called Balata. The solid type is much more durable but tends to be very lively when landing, thus making the short game control very much more difficult; it does not spin nearly as much as the softer ball, which is usually the choice of the good golfer who puts feel, touch and control before durability. This thinner-skinned Balata-covered ball may not fly quite as far as the more solid one but it is easier to spin and control around the green.

Which ball compression? Most of the solid balls have a compression factor of 90-100 which means it will not flatten very much on impact. The softer wound balls are available in 80, 90 and 100 compression. Eighty, being the easiest to flatten at impact, is ideal for ladies and some ageing men. Ninety is ideal for strong women players and medium-hitting male golfers, and the 100 compression golf ball is most suitable for young top-class amateurs and tournament professionals.

It is advisable to use a slightly lower compression ball in the colder winter months. Carry it in your trouser or skirt pocket before teeing off — golf balls perform much better when they are slightly warm!

Whichever ball you choose, stick to it and become accustomed to the feel of it. This is very important, especially in the 'short game'.

Golf balls for seniors

Once again, there are certain golf balls that will help the senior player: Spalding, for example, now produce an oversize ball called the Magna. This ball is very good news for older players as, being bigger, is easier to hit, sits up more on the fairway and, believe it or not, is easier to putt! So again, talk to your professional or coach about the type of ball you should be using to suit your particular game.

GLOSSARY OF GOLFING TERMINOLOGY

Address: the position of your body as you prepare to swing.

Albatross: three stokes under par on a hole.

Aiming: lining-up the clubhead and body in relation to the target.

Alignment: *see* Aiming.

Angle of attack: the angle at which the clubhead approaches the ball on the downswing.

Approach shots: Shots to the green from about 135 yards (120 m).

Back nine: the second nine holes of a golf course.

Backswing: the movement taking the clubhead away from the golf ball.

Birdie: one stroke under par on a hole.

Bobbing: the term used when straightening the knees during the backswing, causing the head to bob up and down.

Bogey: one stroke over par on a hole.

Borrow: the amount you need to aim away from the pin when putting to allow for any slope of the green.

Bunker: a depression through the green mostly partially filled with sand, though such hazards can have an earth or grass surface. The club may not be grounded or full practice swings taken in them.

Chip shot: a low-trajectory and running shot played when close to the green.

Closed stance: the body alignment pointing to the right of the intended target at address for right-handers and to the left for left-handers.

Clubface: the part of the clubhead that strikes the ball.

Cup: the inside lining of the hole (usually made of plastic or metal).

Divot: the piece of turf removed by the clubhead after impact.

Dog-leg: a fairway which bends to right or left and obstructs you from playing directly to the green.

Double bogey: two strokes over par on a hole.

Draw: a ball curving slightly from right to left for right-handers during flight or left to right for left-handers.

Drive: a shot played from a tee, with a long wood or iron.

Driver: a number 1 wood, or metal, used for teeing off.

Eagle: two strokes under par on a hole.

Explosion shot: the shot played from a greenside bunker.

Fade: a ball curving slightly from left to right for right-handers during flight and right to left for left-handers.

Fairway: the area (usually kept well cut) between the tee and the green.

Follow-through: the part of the swing which occurs just after impact.

Fourball: a match in which partners, each playing their own ball, score with the better of their two balls against the better of their opponents' two balls.

Foursome: a match in which two players play against another two players with each side using only one ball and playing alternate shots.

Front nine: the first nine holes of the golf course.

Full set: the Rules of Golf allow a maximum of 14 clubs to be carried.

Green: the putting surface on which the hole is cut.

Greensome: both partners in a fourball tee off, then select which ball they will continue to use, taking alternate shots.

Grip: the part of the golf club you hold; also the method by which you hold the club.

Gross score: the player's total score before the handicap deduction is made.

Halve: to complete the hole in the same score as the opposition in match-play.

Handicap: an adjustable figure given to players according to their playing ability against the standard scratch score of the course.

Hazards: natural or man-made areas usually filled with sand or water; the club cannot be grounded when addressing the ball in these hazards. *Check rules and penalties for dropping out.*

Hook: a shot which curves violently from right to left for right-handers during flight or left to right for left-handers.

In-to-out: the clubhead travelling from inside the ball-to-target line to the outside of it just after impact.

Iron: the metal-headed, bladed golf club with varying loft, ranging from 1 to sand iron.

Lateral water hazard: a water hazard defined by red stakes. *Check penalty and rules for dropping out.*

Lie: the actual angle formed by the shaft and the bottom of the club. Also used to describe how the ball is sitting on the fairway.

Match play: when the result of play is decided by winning or losing holes rather than adding the total strokes played.

Medal play: when the golfer's score is recorded and totalled at the end of the round; also known as Stroke play.

One piece takeaway: the action at the start of the golf swing when arms, hands and clubhead are all moving together.

Open stance: the body alignment pointing to the left of the target for right-handers and to the right for left-handers.

Out of bounds: an area beyond the course, usually marked by white posts, from which it is not permitted to play the ball. *Check penalty rules.*

Out-to-in: the clubhead travelling from outside the ball-to-target line to inside it, just after impact.

Overswing: the point at the top of the backswing when the clubhead drops below horizontal, resulting in loss of control.

Par: the score a good player is expected to achieve on a hole, i.e. 4 shots on a par 4 hole.

Pitch: a high shot to the green from up to about 120 yards (110 m) usually played with 9 iron, pitching wedge or sand wedge.

Pitch mark: the indentation made on the surface of the green when a ball pitches on to it; pitch marks must always be repaired by the player.

Pivot: the turn of the torso in the swing.

Placing: on many courses, particularly during the winter months, players are allowed to clean and move the ball (usually no more than 6 inches (15 cm)) onto a good lie to prevent damaging the course.

Pull: a shot which travels straight during flight but finishes left of the target for a right-hander and right for a left-hander.

Push: the opposite of a pull, caused by the clubhead swinging from inside-out.

Reading the green: studying the line and speed of the green when putting.

Rhythm: the pace of the golf swing which should be unhurried.

Rough: areas of the course that are not closely mown.

Rub of the green: an unfortunate bounce over which the player has no control.

Sand traps: *see* Traps.

Scratch Player: a player with a handicap of nought.

Shank: one of golf's most dreaded shots, resulting in the ball striking the socket of an iron club.

Slice: a shot which curves violently from left to right during flight for right-handers and right to left for left-handers.

Square set-up: when the feet, hips and shoulders are set parallel to the ball-to-target line at address.

Stableford: a competition in which points are awarded in relation to the number of shots a player takes over or under par at each hole; usually 1 point for 1 over par, 2 points for par, 3 points for 1 under par and 4 points for 2 under par, after allowing for handicap; e.g. if a player gets a stroke on a hole and has a gross 4 on a par 3, the player will have a nett 3 and be awarded 2 points.

Standard scratch: the course rating set on a daily basis by the match committee.

Stroke play: *see* Medal play.

Swingweight: The measurement used to match clubs to each other so they feel the same weight when swung. Referred to as a matched set.

Takeaway: the initial part of the back swing.

Target line: the line from the ball to the target.

Through the green: The area between the tee and the green (not hazards), but including the rough.

Topping: when the bottom of the club face contacts the ball, usually on the top half, hammers the ball into the ground resulting in a low, skimming and mostly short shot.

Traps: another name for bunkers.

Turning: the correct movement during the backswing and the downswing.

Up and down: a chip and a putt to sink the ball.

Vardon grip: the overlapping grip originated by the famous golfer, Harry Vardon.

Waggle: the fluid backwards and forwards movement of hands, wrists and clubhead at address.

Water hazard: defined by yellow markers (red markers in the case of a Lateral water hazard). *Check penalty and rules for dropping out.*

Lateral water hazard: defined by red markers (yellow markers in the case of a Water hazard). *Check penalty and rules for dropping out.*

Weight transference: the shifting of the body weight to the back foot on the backswing and then onto the front foot on the downswing.

Wood: a club with a rounded solid back designed primarily for distance and made of either wood, metal or graphite (and other exotic man-made fibres). Today, woods up to 7 loft are increasingly popular.

INDEX

Page numbers in *italics* refer to illustrations.

address (stance) position 15, 16, *16*, 18, 23
alignment 15
— irons *46*
arthritis 13

back problem 34
backswing 25, 34, *38*, *39*
ball
— above feet 93, *93*
— below feet 94, *94*
— choosing 118
— compression 118
— distance from 19, *19*
— flight of 117
— on downhill lie 95, *95*, *96*
— on uphill lie, 95, *95*, *97*
— position 20, *20*, 22
body posture 16, 18, *18*
bunker shots
— buried lie 69, *68*
— fairway bunkers 71
— wet hard-packed sand 71
— normal lie 63, *66*, *67*, *69*, *70*
putting from 71

chipping 73, *78*
— chip and run shot *81*
clubs
— distances 117
— grips 116
— lie 115
— purchasing 115, 116
downswing *27*, 28, *28*, *29*, *29*, *42*
draw (see hook)
driver (see woods)
duffing (see fluffing)

equipment 115

fade (see slice)
fairway bunkers 71
fairway irons *23*
fairway woods 21, *21*, 44
faults 104–111
fluffing 108, *108*
follow-through 30, 31, *31*, *32*, *33*, *39*, *43*

gloves 118
glossary 119
greens 90
— fast 90
— slow 90
— wet 90
grip 9–15
— baseball (double-handed) 8, *12*
— hooker's *13*
— interlocking 8
— overlapping (Vardon) 10, *10*, *11*, *12*
— slicer's *13*
— thickness 118
— weak *12*

hazards 114
hook 106, *106*
— deliberate 102, *103*, *109*
irons
— long 44, *45*
— medium 48
— off the tee 44
— short 48, *48*, *50*, *51*

low shots under trees 99

mental game 112
metal woods 118

percentage shots 111
pitching 73, 75, *76*, *77*, 80
— and run shot *74*, 75, *78*, *79*

posture 16, *16*, 18, *18*
practice 113
professionals 113
pull 107, *107*

putting 83, *88*, *89*, 90, *91*
— borrow of the green 86
— alignment *85*, 86, *86*, *87*
— grip 83, *84*
— drills *61*
— in windy conditions 90
— judging speed 90
— reading the green 90
— stance 83, *84*, *88*, *89*
push 107, *107*

rough
— deep *98*, *98*, 99
— short 99
run shots
— with lofted club 75
— with putter 75

shaft flex 116
shanking 108
skying 108
slice 104, *105*
— deliberate 102, *103*, *109*
sloping lies 93

— ball above feet 93, *93*
— ball below feet 94, *94*
— ball on uphill lie 95, *95*, 97
— ball on downhill lie 95, *95*, *96*
square stance 16, *16*
stance (address) position 15, 18
swing 25, 26, *27*, 28, *28*, 29, *29*, 30, *30*, 31,
   31, *32*, *33*, 34
— drills 55, *56*, *57*, *58*, *59*, *60*
— perfect 34
— plane *49*
— sequence 37

tactics 111
teeing heights *46*
topping 107, *107*
trees
— low shots under 99, *100*
— close to trunks 101, *101*

woods 37, *39*, *41*, *42*, *43*, *52*, *53*
— off the fairway 44
— off the tee 37

CREDITS

Photographs
ALLSPORT UK LTD 7.
G.T. GRANT PHOTOGRAPHY 3, 10(1),
22, 23(b), 52, 52, 63, 69, 80, 81, 84(br), 91.
C.W. GRIFFIN 4, 9(r), 10(r), 11, 12, 17, 18(a),
24, 25, 27, 28, 29, 31, 32, 36, 37, 40, 41, 42,
43, 45, 50, 51, 62, 64, 65, 66, 67, 70, 72, 73,
74, 76, 77, 79, 82, 83, 84(a), 85, 86, 87, 92,
96, 97, 110, 115.
MILLWOOD RESORT 1.

N.Z. PHOTOCORP 2.
GARY PLAYER COMPANY 8.
MICHELE TAYLOR 9(1), 16, 18(b), 19, 21,
23(a), 33, 38, 39, 46, 47, 48, 55, 56, 57, 58,
59, 60, 61, 64, 68, 78, 84(b1), 88, 89, 93, 94,
95, 98, 100, 101, 104, 105, 106, 111.
(a) above; (b) below; (l) left; (r) right.

Illustrations
Mark Roman

Personal Golf Record

Date	Golf Course	Handicap	Score	Course Par	Course Rating	Differential

Personal Golf Record

Date	Golf Course	Handicap	Score	Course Par	Course Rating	Differential

Personal Golf Record

Date	Golf Course	Handicap	Score	Course Par	Course Rating	Differential

Personal Golf Record

Date	Golf Course	Handicap	Score	Course Par	Course Rating	Differential

Personal Golf Record

Date	Golf Course	Handicap	Score	Course Par	Course Rating	Differential